BEYOND SURVIVAL

◇

Creating Prosperity Through People

Robert B. Blaha

AIR ACADEMY PRESS
& ASSOCIATES, LLC

ISBN 1-880156-04-0

Printed in the United States of America
9 8 7 6 5 4 3 2 1 — 98 97 96 95

Published by

AIR ACADEMY PRESS
& ASSOCIATES,LLC

1155 Kelly Johnson Blvd, Suite 105
Colorado Springs, CO 80920
Fax (719) 531-0778
(719) 531-0777
aapa@rmii.com

Contents

Foreword

BEYOND SURVIVAL
Creating Prosperity Through People

The 1990s. "Downsizing," "Rightsizing," "Reengineering," "Breakthrough Thinking," buzzword after buzzword—Result?—A widening gap has been created between leadership and others in the organization. People are coming to work tired and confused. Eight hours (or more) later, they head for home often even more tired and confused.

Beyond Survival is a book that has the answers you need to get more out of yourself and your associates. It will help you get more out of your life than just surviving day after day. Work will become more rewarding and less confusing.

Beyond Survival teaches you how to create prosperity in your work environment. How to feel good about your contributions, and how to impact your team, whether that team has five or 50,000 members. Whether you are in leadership or "just work here," you need to read **Beyond Survival**.

Author Robert B. Blaha takes his almost two decades worth of experience as a human resource and quality pundit for several major companies and transforms his knowledge and experiences into an easy-to-read "how-to" for creating "_Prosperity Through People_." He explains how to make the quality process a rewarding journey.

A final thought for those who might be saying to yourselves, "So, what's new?" **Read this book**. You will soon discover why positive quality results have not occurred the way they should have in your organization. Better yet, you will now know what needs to be done to enable more black ink to be added to the bottom line!

The frontier of organizational success is only available to those who have the will and way to explore it. Join the journey—Welcome to _Beyond Survival_.

Preface

The employees in an organization are its most valuable assets. If they don't feel involved in and rewarded by their work, their commitment to the organization will be minimal.

A High Performance Work System (HPWS) is a focused, yet flexible, way of involving every employee in managing the organization to high levels of achievement in order to maintain a competitive advantage.

The implementation of HPWS can move an organization from a state of lackluster performance and poor employee morale to one of healthy bottom line and highly motivated team members striving to meet customer needs.

HPWS can, when implemented within a single department in an organization, bring about a positive change in what people think about their jobs; generate interest in improving the service they provide; and promote pride in the organization they work for.

What is this HPWS that it can affect overall corporate health and promote in employees a sense of ownership for quality and pride in a job well done?

This book tells the story of HPWS. It compares this innovative approach to that of management by traditional methods; explains the steps involved in developing a HPWS; and describes some of the tools available to assist in the data gathering phases of this process. It can help your organization (and you as a part of it) move *beyond survival* and create prosperity in the work place.

A clear understanding of the organization's history (Chapter 1) establishes its behavioral starting point for the journey into High Performance Work Systems. This step is followed by the gaining of awareness of what High Performance Work Systems are and what they do (Chapter 2), and the importance of carefully structuring work teams (Chapter 3).

These activities will point to opportunities that can be classified and worked as the business case and focus for this group's HPWS knowledge (Chapter 4). The organization can now compare the opportunities offered by its current work system with those afforded by a High Performance Work System and decide whether to proceed (Chapter 5).

Note: The decision made at this juncture is critical since it requires a change in individual and group behavior. The change will require teamwork, collaboration, and commitment on the part of all participants.

The next step involves developing a long-range vision of measurable behavioral characteristics to which the organization aspires (Chapter 6). This vision becomes the bull's-eye at which the HPWS will aim. It must align with the entities' values.

Progressing toward this long-range vision also requires creating a transitional growth plan that is engineered in a measurable 3-Point Alignment process involving all roles in the organization (Chapter 7). It is through this process that the HPWS comes to life.

Implementation of individual and group growth plans (Chapter 8) launches the organization on its HPWS journey.

Once it's implemented, the HPWS will continually evolve and require continuous support. By its very nature, it is flexible and responsive to change. This progress toward the vision encompasses feedback and continuous checking for alignment of all elements in the process (Chapter 9).

The last chapter (Chapter 10) discusses tools for designing, applying, and interpreting measurement systems to the High Performance Work System process.

————Acknowledgements

As I thought of all who have been crucial in completing this project (it was a project!) the list became frightening.

First to my family:

Thanks, Susan (my wife) and Kids (our seven children) for enduring a frustrating time; between building our new home, "the book" and balancing family priorities—"I love you guys!"

To all those who contributed:

Jim Davis, Bill Easter, Bruce Felton, Ed Ferris, Hoyt Fitzsimmons, Cory Guenter, Joyce Kennedy, Jan Kreminski, Jim Oates, Ed Robertson, Marty Storm, Nanci Waniewski, and a host of clients and colleagues—"you're appreciated!"

To my editors Susan Darby and Ed Robertson (text) and Beatriz Orozco (technical lay-out) whose expertise was so needed—we did it!

To our publisher Air Academy Press & Associates and printer and binder R. R. Donnelley & Sons Company—thank you for a quality product.

Thanks to the Muir Agency, especially Bernard Sandoval for the design of the cover—the majesty of the Colorado mountains challenges us to move *Beyond Survival!*

And finally ...

If the book does well—to God be the honor!

Author

Robert B. Blaha has almost twenty years of experience dealing with Human Resources and High Performance Work Systems in senior positions with four major corporations—Ford, Monsanto, Engelhard, and Asea Brown Boveri (ABB). He has authored numerous articles on High Performance Work and is an internationally sought speaker on involvement and cultural change mechanisms.

In 1993 he founded Human Capital Associates (HCA) and serves as the company's President. HCA was created after carefully analyzing why Total Quality and Human Resource initiatives were not working the way organizations thought they should. Robert uses that knowledge to help organizations create effective processes and programs to *"create competitive advantage through people."*

Following the creation of Human Capital Associates, he moved the company to Colorado Springs, Colorado, where he resides with his wife, Susan, and their seven children, on "Seven Arrows Ranch."

Introduction

GUIDING PRINCIPLES

On the sultry morning of July 15, 1789, after peasants had sacked the Bastille, King Louis XVI surveyed the damage and asked one of his courtiers, "Is it a revolt?" "No, sire," the courtier replied. "It is a revolution."

There has never been a decade as challenging or competitive as the 1990s. And, as we move toward the year 2000, companies intent on long-term survival and growth must make dramatic and even revolutionary changes. Those that don't are doomed to fail long before the century turns.

Most major organizations are going through a period of transition. They are reestablishing missions and values. They are restructuring and streamlining their organizations, and pushing Total Quality into their operations. They are attempting to position themselves to create new opportunities and make the most of them.

Now, the time has come for these organizations to accelerate the push to become truly world-class. The best way to accomplish this is through High Performance Work Systems (HPWS).

Make no mistake: High Performance Work Systems will revolutionize the way things are done. While "employee involvement" became key to success in the 1980s and early 1990s, High Performance Work Systems goes well beyond that time frame. Now, teams are established and responsibility for the product or service is placed in the hands of those people who actually do the work. Work teams are self-managed and the manager must assume the new role as trainer, coach, and facilitator.

It is a system that puts the responsibility for customer satisfaction on those people who know the products and services best!

The success of High Performance Work Systems depends on total commitment, trust, empowerment, open and honest communication, and clear, quantitative goals. It requires much more than catch phrases and buzzwords!

Total commitment means just that—commitment at all levels of the organization. Senior management must be willing to invest the time, finances, and resources necessary to make HPWS work. Management must educate itself thoroughly in the philosophy and methodologies of High Performance and begin the formal process of making it happen throughout the organization. The workforce must take responsibility for learning what HPWS is about by building teams and acquiring the capabilities that are at the heart of the HPWS experience. Organizations must have a commitment to <u>fundamentally change</u> the way they operate from top to bottom!

Trust is also a major ingredient. To succeed, HPWS needs a steady flow of information required to do the job. That means management must trust people with sensitive information to successfully accomplish the task. People must be familiar with balance sheets, profit and loss statements, and other data—information previously considered to be "need to know" information only.

As for empowerment, management must allow people to assume ownership of their positions. With HPWS, employees take a personal interest in improving the organization and its performance.

Communication is the glue that holds it all together. Team members need to understand the goals they're working toward and believe the goals are worth pursuing. For this to happen, the goals must be clearly communicated and actively discussed. All members must be totally open with each other.

Beyond Survival: Creating Prosperity Through People gives you the essentials you need to begin implementing High Performance Work Systems in your organization. It takes you through a succession of logical stages, from awareness through education, to gaining commitment, and finally to implementation. The book contains success stories, and helpful guidance on the pitfalls to be avoided. In addition, there are references to publications that address many of the skills and methodologies that are at the heart of HPWS.

Creating High Performance Work Systems is not easy. If it were, organizations would have already fully implemented the process and reaped the benefits from this *distinct competitive advantage*. If done effectively, HPWS will create enormous power within the enterprise, make coming to work more enjoyable, significantly improve the bottom line, and create prosperity for the future.

Chapter 1

UNDERSTANDING THE ORGANIZATION'S HISTORY

> *"Those who don't remember the past are condemned to repeat it."*
> —*George Santayana*

Before reincarnating itself as a High Performance Work System, an organization needs to take careful stock of where it is now and where it has been. There are many reasons for "why we are what we are." Before an organization can work on the future, it must know and understand its past.

This chapter provides the organization with some guidelines for establishing its baseline and analyzing the root cause of its current values, behaviors, and perceptions.

HIGHLIGHTS:

- Determining where you are and how you got there (reflecting both management and labor history and focusing on changes that occurred along the way)

- Establishing a starting-point for the HPWS journey

- Keeping track of the group's own High Performance Work Systems development experience for later evaluation so that others can learn from it

- Involving the entire organization early on in a non-threatening experience that's programmed for success

CONTENT: The importance of learning from one's history cannot be overemphasized. Since each passing moment becomes history, we are continually shaped and moved by forces both internal and external that must be understood and exploited if we are to continue growing. And while every organization's history is unique, certain elements are common to all.

What the organization needs, then, is a firm grasp on where it is and how it got there. When you know exactly how high up the mountain you've climbed, it's a lot easier to figure out how much further you have to go to reach the top.

That clear retrospective view becomes a baseline for pursuing and measuring future growth. This becomes particularly helpful as a business case for movement toward High Performance Work Systems is put together in Chapter 4 and an evaluation of the present work system occurs in Chapter 5.

ALL THINGS CONSIDERED

While there is no hard-and-fast procedure for conducting a historical analysis, there are a number of elements that should be examined (and addressed) when thinking historically:

- The broad history of the organization, including all its participants and factions (Who and what shaped the past?)

- The processes and procedures previously implemented that affect current activities

- Business, technological, social, and cultural changes and their impact on each other

- Relevant external factors, such as government regulations, economic trends, world events, politics, society, market developments, product requirements, etc. (Have any of these altered the organization's course?)

- All relevant internal factors, such as labor-management relations, organizational design, leader/follower relationships, accountability structures, knowledge, workers, etc.

- The underlying causes of major events such as acquisitions, divestitures, expansion, contractions, unionizations, right sizing, re-engineering, physical catastrophes, etc.

- A "who's who" of organizational "heroes" and "villains" and how they acquired these labels

- Cause-and-effect relationships between attitudinal changes and historical events

- Past "drivers" of change and how they might be useful in the future

- The way decision-making changed as the organization evolved

Although a necessity, examining the organization's history can be rewarding and fun. As a first step on the high road to becoming a High Performance Work System, it offers an easy way for the organization to involve all its people and to gain support for the process.

Keep in mind, however, that you can break your arm trying to pat yourself on the back so early in the process. To be worthwhile, historical self-examination must be unflinchingly honest. Self-congratulation will get you nowhere.

Summary

To repeat, before recasting itself as a High Performance Work System, an organization needs to take careful stock of **where it is now and where it has come from**—and how its own history parallels the overall development of the company. That historical self-awareness becomes the starting point for the transition to HPWS. Keep in mind, too, that as the organization moves toward the HPWS approach, history is being made. Be sure to record it carefully for later use and analysis.

Chapter 2

AWARENESS OF HIGH PERFORMANCE WORK SYSTEMS

"The only constant is change."
—Heraclitus

Change is what this book is about—radical, revolutionary change. But which organizational characteristics, specifically, will be altered as a company progresses toward High Performance Work Systems?

More to the point, just what is a High Performance Work System? What does it look like? What does it do? Why is it needed? And, how does it differ from conventional work units? This chapter examines the main characteristics of High Performance Work Systems and the principles on which they are founded.

HIGHLIGHTS:

- What HPWS means

- What HPWS does not mean

- Characteristics of a HPWS team

- How the HPWS design contrasts with that of a conventional work unit

- The evolution from conventional work unit to HPWS

- HPWS definitions and evaluative statements covering all organizational elements

WHAT HPWS MEANS:

- It is a focused, yet flexible, way of involving every member in managing the organization to High Performance over the long term.

- Decision-making and accountability reside where it makes most sense—at levels where the information is available and client contact and relationships take place.

- Management evolves from bosses into facilitators, guides, and trainers. Rather than give orders, they set work boundaries and facilitate group and interpersonal processes. Instead of hoarding authority, they empower groups and individuals as appropriate, allowing them to function with responsible initiative.

- Recognition and reward systems are designed to encourage the continuous growth, development, and performance of individuals and groups that contribute to achieving the vision of the organization.

- It reflects a shared recognition that business and work climates are constantly changing and that change can be successfully influenced and managed by the organization.

- The essential work system behaviors and work climates are modeled from the top down.

- It is a *proven and documented* approach that many organizations have already used successfully—one that builds on failures as well as on triumphs of many high-involvement applications.

- Goals and action plans are developed and accomplished *continuously* and by all levels.

- Patience and commitment are visibly evident from management.

- The organization succeeds or fails on the strength of its members' commitment.

- Management must set expectations that focus the organization's work.

- Information is provided to enhance performance and tell the organization how its members are performing.

- Traditional management techniques and programs must be evaluated in terms of how well they fit and facilitate the team-building process.

- Training to improve skills is essential.

WHAT HPWS DOES NOT MEAN:

- Bottom-line results don't matter.

- Management gives up its responsibility to manage and all decisions are made by the team.

- Order yields to confusion, and quick-fixes replace careful goal-setting and planning.

- A permissive "feel-good-be-happy" atmosphere prevails, where members do as they please and the results don't matter.

- Group decisions are made by popular vote.

- It is a system for work that is simple and redundant, requiring hands, not minds.

- It's another organizational "fad" or program of the month.

- The organization is without rules governing empowerment.

HIGH PERFORMANCE WORK SYSTEMS ORGANIZATIONAL CHARACTERISTICS

To fully embrace HPWS, an awareness of what changes are being committed to is paramount. What does a HPWS entity look like? How does it operate? Can the organization commit to the philosophy? From a general viewpoint, what characteristics are present?

PHILOSOPHY: Mutual trust and respect, compassion, empowerment, equity, job security, and social and technical integration through teamwork result in individuals feeling responsible for success.

MISSION: Customers are the highest priority. Common goals reflect the primary focus on customers. Total customer satisfaction *must* be key.

JOB DESIGN: (NO FUNCTIONAL SILOS, PLEASE.) Job design is shared, meaningful, flexible, and broad.

TECHNOLOGY: Leading-edge technology supports—but doesn't drive—human efforts.

STRUCTURE: The organization is built around empowered work units which are semi-autonomous and which become self-directed. Members' highly participative involvement and representation in the decision-making process translate into commitment.

ROLES: Roles are mutually supportive, needs-driven, flexible, and clearly understood.

REWARD SYSTEM: Rewards are driven by meeting customer requirements and bottom-line performance. There is equitable sharing of risks and rewards. Shared-goal setting must trigger and promote a sense of ownership.

RECOGNITION: Recognition is used to reinforce desired behavioral change.

COMMUNICATION: Open communication must happen in all directions, and an information system that reaches all employees must be in place. For credibility, good *and* bad news must be shared.

DEVELOPMENT: Training is functional and application-based and must meet individual, team, and customer needs from a social, technical, and business point of view. Job enrichment and career growth are fostered through continual learning.

HIRING TRANSFERS: Over time teams become responsible for selecting their own members.

SYMBOLS: Individual status symbols are minimized; team building, total organization values, and beliefs take center stage.

PERSONNEL GUIDELINES: These are minimal, behaviorally stated, needs-driven, and focused on win/win. They must be based on trust, compassion, and commitment to corporate values and beliefs.

ENVIRONMENT: All employees are tuned into, concerned with, and knowledgeable about, the business environment. The involvement increases with more unification.

The contrast between a traditional organization and one driven toward high performance can be stark. Understanding what traits are present will enable a thorough perspective of the contrasts.

RESEARCH-BASED ORGANIZATION DESIGN CONTRASTS

Traditional Design	High Performance Design
Work centers around the individual	Work centers around the group
Orientation is independent	Orientation is interdependent
Leadership is directive	Leadership is participative (situational)
Pay for specific job classification	Pay for ability and performance
System orientation is technical	System orientation is a balance of the social and technical
Management is a many-layered thing	Management is flat
Work environment is information-poor	Work environment is information-rich
Senior managers are responsible for results	Everyone is responsible for results
Decisions are made at the top	Decisions are made at the "action" level
Focus is internal	Focus is external and internal

Traditional Design	**High Performance Design**
Operations are built around large units	Operations are built around small units
Specialization is king	Multifunctionalism reigns
Cooperation is rare	Cooperation is everywhere
Status is based on one's position	Status is based on one's contributions
Rule is dictatorial	Decision-making is shared
Mistakes are punished	Mistakes teach - coaching, counseling prevails
Differences are ignored	Differences are valued as resources
Change is resisted	Change is welcomed and driven by customer needs
Training is sporadic (a cost)	Training is continuous (an investment)
Learning is passive	Learning is active (through involvement)
The product is everything	The product is important, but the customer is most important
Organization values are unclear	Organization values clear and connected to objectives
Managers control work	Managers manage information, employees manage work
Bottom-line focus by a few	Bottom-line focus by all
Organization supports management	Organization supports employees' focus on customer

Another way to view this process of change is from a continuum viewpoint (see Figure 2-1). In this illustration, a number of systems are examined from a maturity standpoint (crawl to run), illustrating the process towards HPWS.

CONVENTIONAL SYSTEMS - - - - - - > HIGH PERFORMANCE WORK SYSTEMS

AREA	CRAWL	WALK	JOG	RUN
Management	• Quality, a necessary end • Problem detection/sorting	• Quality, a cost	• Quality, an economic imperative • Resources to prevention	• Quality, a superordinate value • Prevention-way of life
Organization	• Vertical Management • QC - the policeman	• Matrix • QA has quality responsibility but little authority	• AD hoc problem-solving teams • Quality responsibility deployed to line functions	• Teams and focused factories • All employees responsible for quality
System/Measurement	• QC manuals • No quality costs	• QA policy/established • Quality costs gathered	• QA system established/implemented/audited • Self-inspection	• Continuous, never-ending improvement • Intangible quality costs attached
Tools	• Data pollution, little analysis • No SPC	• 7 QC tools • Elementary control charts	• Design of experiments (DOE) • SPC: pre control	• Design DOE • Six Sigma metrics (in place)
Customer	• Profit over customer satisfaction • Voice of the engineer dominates	• Customer inputs sought • Customer measurements started	• Voice of the customer researched through quality function deployment, conjoint analysis, etc.	• Customer enthusiasm • Next operation as "customer" pervades the organization
Design	• "Toss over the wall" to production • Concentration only on performance parameters	• Eng/Mfg. teams for new products • Some collaboration	• Design for manufacturability • Accelerated life tests	• Design for zero variation and zero failures • User-friendly built-in diagnostics
Supplier	• Adversarial relationships • Table—pound for price	• Start of mutual trust and reduced supplier base	• Partnership suppliers • Sole suppliers	• Supplier an extension of company • Self-certified suppliers
Process/Manufacturing	• High scrap, rework • Poor yields	• 80-90% yield • Quality metrics in place	• Total defects/unit measurement	• Scrap eliminated • Insp./test greatly reduced
Support Services	• Poor quality, high cost, long cycle time • No measurements	• Next Operation as Customer concept introduced • Steering committee, process owners, and improvement teams established	• Internal customers measure internal supplier performance • Quality, cost, and cycle time improvement tools used	• Internal customer evaluation replace boss evaluation • Financial incentives/penalities established
People	• People - pair of hands • Management overbearing • No training	• Quality circles • Management still not involved with people • Sporadic training	• Management participatory • "Rewards" changed • Training implemented on the job with measured results	• "Every employee a manager" • Workers empowered • From management to leadership

Figure 2-1

Summary

In its purposes, structure, and defining characteristics, HPWS differs radically from conventional approaches to management and organizational structure. Where conventional work settings emphasize individual enterprise, direct rule, and a multi-layered management, HPWS stresses group dynamics, participatory decision-making, and flat management structures.

Before attempting to reorganize along high performance lines, it is essential to understand what HPWS is—and isn't. That understanding is a prelude to identifying the key ingredients of HPWS success—the subject of Chapter 3.

Chapter 3

KEY INGREDIENTS

"I couldna done it without my players. "
—Casey Stengel, on being congratulated
for managing the Yankees to a pennant.

A High Performance Work System is possible only with well-trained and empowered people. But what are the critical factors in making a High Performance Work Group come together and succeed?

This chapter defines the basis of HPWS success in a variety of work situations. An essential element of that success is the endorsement and participation of leadership which must set the direction and focus for the group.

HIGHLIGHTS: High Performance Work Groups are based on proven behavioral management principles. These principles become the core of the flexible work system that results from a combination of factors such as shared visions, common purposes, well-defined boundaries, and a culture that is achievement-oriented and supportive.

Figure 3-1 is a graphical representation of the evolution of traditional work into a High Performance Work status.

Step 1: Business as usual. The supervisor is the central authority to whom the members look for direction, decisions, approval, rewards, and recognition. When it is necessary to interface with other departments, the supervisor is the contact.

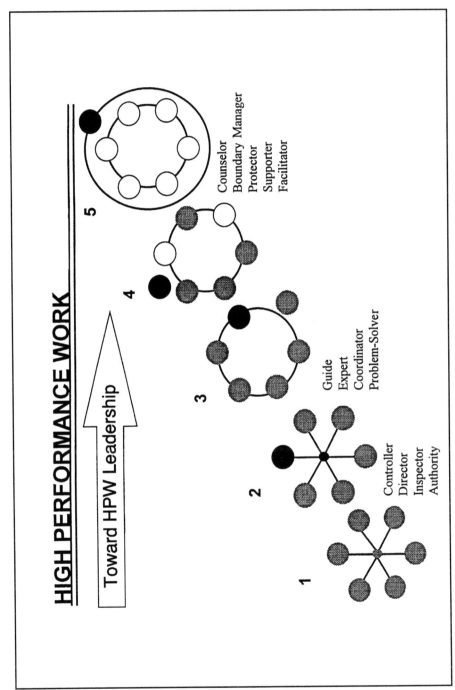

Figure 3-1

HIGHLIGHTS (CONT.)

Step 2: After "basic" training in handling interpersonal conflicts and conducting effective meetings, the members agree on why they should function as a group. They establish ground rules and norms that support group principles and open communication. The supervisor's role becomes less directive.

Step 3: Acting as group members, the facilitator and leader begin to transfer power, information, and expectations to the other members and help open communication channels among team members. The idea is to eliminate choke points and keep communication simple, direct, and unencumbered.

Step 4: Having developed leadership skills and redefined roles, members assume some of the traditional supervisory and planning skills and become more self-managing.

Step 5: The supervisor's role has evolved into a facilitator, counselor, coach, and boundary manager. The team will now require support and input for strategic direction but will be empowered to operate as self-managing. The supervisory/facilitator span of influence begins to broaden.

NOTE: Although organizations are experimenting with "leaderless" concepts (i.e., no management), direction and correct focus are a must!

CONTENT: The characteristics of a High Performance Work Group, including the functions it typically assumes, are discussed in this chapter.

You can't make it up as you go along. Scope is defined by mission and goals as aligned with those of the organization. If the team is to succeed, formal organization guidelines and behavioral standards are essential as is *leadership participation* in *defining expectations* for the team.

High Performance Groups work! Their efficacy has been proven and documented time and again in a number of forward-looking companies. As companies attempt to move *beyond survival* over the next few years, they must make High Performance Groups work for them. That happens when people buy into the High Performance System concept, with committed leadership guiding the way.

Self-management

It is crucial that members understand up-front the current state of the business as well as the rationale for focusing on specific markets, customers, and objectives. Following that, the transfer of authority is the next step toward empowerment. The group will make some decisions independently and others jointly and accept recommendations in matters beyond its scope. The clear definition of these parameters will aid in the transfer of responsibility, authority, and ownership to the group.

The transition to self-management requires careful planning and a definite structure; otherwise members simply won't know what is expected of them. Teams also need a purpose and mission which members must understand. Indeed, their every action and decision must be guided by a commitment to the purpose and mission.

Development and training are a must, especially in such performance-based skills as problem solving, process mapping, benchmarking, meetings management, and interactive skills.

Of course, no HPWS initiative can be effective unless management is serious about delegating control functions. Management has responsibility for setting direction, establishing expectations, and providing focus and support. It *cannot abdicate this responsibility*. If management wavers, the system will collapse. It's as simple as that!

It is management that gives the group its original charge and sets the determinants for success. Input from leadership, based on these measures, will reflect improved performance by the group.

These management-defined metrics tend to be more generic than those used by the group, which are directed toward solving specific problems and defined by the group during the goal-setting process. Traditional measurements will not be adequate as the group expands beyond work standards and addresses the total cycle. Organizational wide metrics can serve as macro-indicators of success, but the individual work group will define specific customer-related success factors.

Empowerment

Real worker empowerment is still a relatively new concept in many workplaces. It is established by creating a measure of trust between management and the group, helping members to develop and use their skills and knowledge. The give-and-take of setting a mission, goals, and action plan to support management's charge to the group is essential to empowerment.

That's not to say it will always be easy. The sharing of control and closely-held information is painful to many who have come to see these intangibles as their base of power. If management takes the lead in the information sharing process, the group's empowerment will be greatly enhanced. Empowerment requires creating an environment where groups are willing to take risks within defined boundaries, grow, and take responsibility. *But they must have leadership's backing to do so.*

Structure

It should not be inferred from this book that traditional work teams—the kind that prevail right now—are without value. On the contrary, these work teams, just like High Performance Groups, demand continuous cooperation among employees moving toward common objectives. Typically, the objective is a specific core business process such as "customer order to engineering" or "drafting."

Traditional work groups are also conducive to training and continuous improvement. But, unlike High Performance, traditional work teams tend to be run autocratically, with a single boss providing direction.

Traditional work teams are usually content with the status quo. But, their comfort level goes a long way towards easing the passage into the "brave new world of High Performance Work Systems."

Some multifunctional groups have extended life cycles and thus qualify as traditional work teams. Most teams don't, however, because they are geared to a specific project or problem. It is the continuity of training and experience that makes natural work groups the best candidates for the High Performance approach. They serve as a useful training ground.

Scope

Research indicates that groups work best with 8-12 members; outside of that range, the likelihood of success diminishes. **Reason**: *teams must be small enough to allow participation, cross-training, and interdependence, and large enough to encompass the required range of skills.* Size can conflict with teamwork when it impedes the flow of information or the building of relationships.

Management as Sponsor

It is worth repeating here that management has a pivotal role to play in actively sponsoring the transition to the High Performance approach. It is management's responsibility to alert members to the fact that it's no longer business as usual. Management will also be called on to help members fit into their new roles, and to eliminate arbitrary and unnecessary constraints. Simply stated, management's role is tougher. The mix of focus, information and development requires constant attention and re-evaluation.

Mission and Goals

High Performance Groups are focused on success. To achieve success, they need a well-defined mission—one that the members all agree upon, and that management views as consistent with business objectives.

It is this mission that drives the group forward; it's the central element in the High Performance process. To make the mission statement understandable and quantifiable, it should be broken down into small segments that members can relate to given their personal experiences. The group can then formulate long- and short-term goals and measurable action plans to support the mission and to provide an active map of requirements by which to gauge their progress (see Figure 3-2). (In-process measures are important to achieve expectations and monitor progress.)

The essence of effective teamwork is linking and balancing individual and group success. True employee ownership is achieved through effective teamwork.

ELEVEN THINGS HIGH PERFORMANCE GROUPS ALWAYS DO

There is no master list to identify every activity for HPWS. However, there are a number of activities that are constant across organizations who move towards HPWS groups.

Set Goals

After drafting a mission statement, the group establishes its long-range goals as well as a preliminary action plan for achieving them.

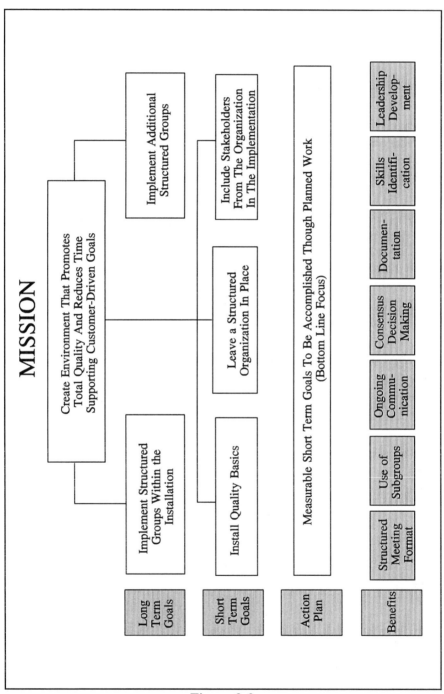

Figure 3-2

This is done through the use of basic processes such as brainstorming, cause analysis, data gathering, problem solving, and group consensus. The group's goals, together with the charge they receive from management, provide a sense of whether progress is being made toward the vision.

Focus on the Customer

High Performance Work Groups serve both internal and external customers. Far more closely attuned to the needs of both groups, and benefiting from enhanced linkages and communication, High Performance Work achieves much higher levels of customer satisfaction than traditional work. The groups regularly solicit feedback from stakeholders, specifically customers, and use it to carefully tailor products and services to market demand.

Plan and Schedule Work

It becomes the group's responsibility to schedule work. Members learn to do this using flow charts, streamlining work processes through the use of Just-in-Time scheduling, Kanban material ordering (if manufacturing), and point-of-use storage. Their own personal awareness of glitches in the existing process can also be utilized to achieve "quick hits" in productivity improvement.

The planning and scheduling effort makes full use of all available resources—people, equipment, facilities, and information. It also implies an important division of labor: *people do what people do best* and *computers do what computers do best.*

Define Their Own Roles

Members discover early on that many, if not most, traditional job descriptions are either obsolete or too restrictive for the process as it has been redefined. It will be up to the group—with management's backing—to modify roles, redefine others, and redistribute the work load.

As boundaries are redefined and greater authority is accepted, management's commitment to change will quickly become apparent. As new roles are identified, it is essential that management begin to share control and reevaluate overly restrictive policies and procedures.

Make Decisions by Consensus

Members of a High Performance Group don't compete against each other; there are no winners and losers. To achieve this state, the group must agree that most decisions will be made by consensus. No one person has control over decision making.

Of course, consensus is possible only when there is open discussion of concerns, and where members can express themselves freely with no fear of reproach. In the end, not every member of the group will be happy with the chosen action. But they must all be able to support the group in achieving the desired outcome. Again, the impetus to operate by consensus must come from management. Interactive skills and effective meeting tools become crucial for success.

Find Solutions

With proper training and support, the group will brainstorm, analyze, measure, and solve problems that would previously have been the responsibility of management. Total Quality training, covering such skills as Statistical Process Control (SPC), will be extremely helpful in this regard.

Even in conventional work settings, employees develop their own problem-solving methods which they continually test and refine on the job; it's an intrinsic part of the work experience. To gel as High Performance, members must continually establish and sharpen techniques for solving problems as a group—especially those problems that pit individual needs against business priorities. As the group becomes conversant, Total Quality tools can greatly impact the ability of the group to explain and document solutions. These tools, which range from brainstorming to scatter diagrams, prioritization matrices, and process mapping, are now widely used and taught in most organizations. They are described in detail in Chapter 10.

Interface with Others

Management serves as a kind of "emissary" to other functions during the early development of a HPW Group. As training progresses, this linkage function will be increasingly taken on by the group itself, diminishing the need for outside help in communications and training.

Measure Results

High Performance Groups are continually measuring their own performance. Is the group on track and moving forward? Does the group effectively address management's charge? (See Chapter 10 for techniques for measuring behaviors and results.)

It's important to keep a broad perspective in selecting which measurements to apply. Even so, the initial goals and measurements will invariably need to be expanded as the group moves from one stage to the next. This metric development process never ends. (Figure 3-3 is an example of a group measurement that demonstrates one element of group performance.)

Evaluate Each Other

As a group matures, the members develop a strong concern for success. They feel responsible for how they perform and will frequently request the authority to evaluate each other—as an input to supervision, peer counseling, and cross-training.

Members need feedback about the effects of their behavior on each other, and on the group's efforts. Peer evaluation is thus a crucial part of employee empowerment. It provides group members with an indispensable tool for improving their performance.

CYCLE TIME (ACTUAL EXAMPLE)
IN WORK DAYS

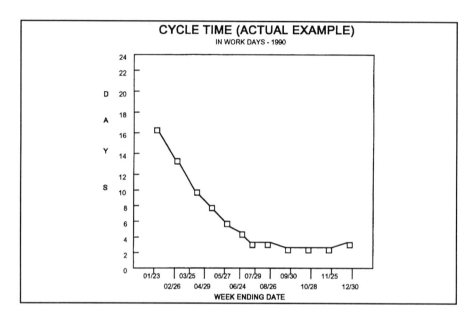

QUALITY ISSUES

- Push system

- Poor communication between assembly and test

- Physically separated processes

- Dedicated assembly stations

ACTIONS

- Re-lay out area to bring assembly and test together

- Establish a quality feedback process

- Develop universal assembly stations

- Actively pursue cross-training

- Establish queue table pull system

Figure 3-3

Since responsibilities are shared, members become very familiar with real role requirements. They're aware, far more clearly than non-members, of just how well they're doing—and which members need closer supervision. Of course, the very notion of peer evaluation will be new to many members, and they will require training to be able to channel effective criticism. (See Chapter 10 for evaluation ideas.)

Select Members

In most cases, members are initially selected by management, with members having little say in team composition. Where there is more than one team in an area, a steering committee may assign members to the teams based on skill, knowledge, and experience levels.

Often, when employees are exposed to real teamwork, a few find they simply cannot adapt to the concept and find that the best option is to look for new employment. As the group advances, the employees' departure provides a lesson in the skill of structured interviewing, since those remaining will select additional members. They will have the job of evaluating the employee's skills and other qualifications to determine if he or she is right for the team. It's a way of getting the empowerment process to a "real time" situation.

Manage Conflicts

In traditional, hierarchical organizations, employees are rewarded for suppressing conflict. In a High Performance setting, conflict is seen as necessary and must be managed and valued.

Suppression of conflict makes it impossible to resolve problems and hidden agendas that hamper effectiveness. The meeting process and sharing of leadership are the beginning steps in managing conflicts and creating a mutually supportive environment. Alternative evaluation and listening skills enhancement are more advanced examples of conflict resolution.

FIVE THINGS HIGH PERFORMANCE ORGANIZATIONS ALMOST NEVER DO

Deviant behavior must be discouraged and eliminated. In HPWS certain activities cannot be allowed.

Play It by Ear

Some may get the idea that High Performance is a kind of free-wheeling discussion where rules are non-existent and members enjoy carte blanche to "do their own thing."

Wrong!

A High Performance organization is as painstakingly designed as a space satellite. It has a carefully articulated mission, goals and objectives, and an action plan to keep it on track. Freedom reigns, but rules abound. While many antiquated hierarchical conventions will be modified or discarded, High Performance does not operate independently of existing contracts, structures, and controls, and members are bound by established procedures.

Vote

High Performance organizations do not determine actions by vote; voting only produces winners and losers and does nothing to rally the entire group behind an action. Rather, they act by consensus. Once a decision is made, all members are committed to support it, regardless of personal opinions.

Decision by consensus is the *sine qua non* of High Performance Work Systems. Achieving a consensus requires that ample time be spent in any decision-making process to elicit all views and enlist the support of members. Everyone doesn't have to like a decision, but the process must insure that all are pledged to support it.

Suppress Conflict

There is no place for factionalism in High Performance, but that isn't to say that conflict is suppressed. Far from it. Conflicts are often the basis of vigorous discussions, new information, and sound decisions. But members must be developed in the art of conflict management and resolution. The truth is, conflicts are inevitable in any solution situation, work-related or otherwise. The High Performance groups learn and grow from conflicts—they do not sweep them under the rug. Fact-based management techniques, along with the use of proven problem-solving techniques, can go a long way toward resolving conflict.

Overlook Training

To do so would be foolhardy. High Performance Groups cannot function without constant guidance, training, and retraining.

Develop at the Same Pace

No two groups develop at the same pace. All groups go through "forming, storming, norming, and performing" states as they evolve from a collection of individuals into a smoothly functioning and effective team. The real questions are: *Is the group focused on the right issues?* and *Does management support the process?*

HOW THEY FUNCTION

Having covered the foundation concepts, it is now important to begin to understand "specific" ingredients that drive High Performance Work Systems.

GROUND RULES AND NORMS

The group must establish ground rules for behavior in and out of meetings. A sample set of ground rules is shown in Figure 3-4.

SAMPLE GROUND RULES FOR A HIGH PERFORMANCE GROUP

Definition:
A ground rule requires total adherence by every member without exception. When a ground rule is broken, correction measures should be taken immediately.

1. Show respect for the opinions and ideas of others and for each team member as a person.
2. Listen to suggestions before criticizing them.
3. Agree on and prepare a written agenda for team meetings.
4. Everyone has an equal voice; do not interrupt.
5. Reach decisions by group consensus.
6. Be on time for meetings.
7. Be prepared to postpone a decision until everyone agrees by the next meeting.
8. Reserve the last five minutes of each meeting for critiquing the meeting and setting next meeting's agenda.
9. Establish time limits and follow them for each team meeting. (Appoint timekeeper.)
10. Require a quorum to hold a meeting.

Adapted from Structured Teamwork ® *Performance Resources, Inc., Austin, Texas*

Figure 3-4

Ground rules are basic axioms of appropriate behavior that all members must observe at all times: listen before criticizing, be on time for meetings, etc. Should a ground rule be violated, the meeting should be stopped and the violation addressed.

Ground rules are normally based on members' thinking and on the experience of previous teams. While some ground rules are virtually universal, others will vary according to the personality of members.

Norms, on the other hand, provide a tool for encouraging and checking desired behavior; they guide rather than dictate.   For example, "Constructive criticism is welcome."

A violation of a norm does not necessarily bring the meeting to a halt or demand immediate action.   Consider #2 in the sample norms on Figure 3-5: "Members are to be open to criticism of ideas without being offended."   There is clearly no urgency to stop the meeting and apply corrective measures the moment a member takes umbrage at a critical comment; should the norm be ignored repeatedly, however, the group will want to discuss it to get themselves back on track and assure the highest performance levels.

SAMPLE NORMS FOR A HIGH PERFORMANCE GROUP

Definition:
A norm can be viewed as a behavioral guideline or expectation of how members will treat or respond to each other.   Unlike ground rule violations, the occasional norm infraction will not necessarily require immediate action.

(Examples Only - to be completed by teams)

1.   Complaints and gripes are to be left outside the meeting. Constructive criticism is welcome.
2.   Members should be open to criticism of their ideas without being offended.
3.   Attendance at team meetings is crucial.   Members are responsible for notifying the team leader when they expect to be absent.
4.   Team members should observe all ground rules and norms while in their work environment.
5.   Participation from all members should be encouraged.

Adapted from Structured Teamwork® Performance Resources, Inc., Austin, Texas

---

Figure 3-5

The Meeting Process

There's no magic to developing an efficient meeting format such as the one shown in Figure 3-6; it's largely a matter of common sense. But it provides the frame for virtually all communications and is a prerequisite to High Performance, since the discipline of the meeting process invariably carries over into daily work situations.

How often should a group meet? That depends on how much new information needs to be shared and how much interaction members have during the course of the work week. As a rule, routine meetings are needed, even after the HPWS process is firmly established. But, the *length of meetings decreases dramatically as member communications skills improve.*

SAMPLE MEETING FORMAT

LEADER: Recorder from last session

RECORDER: Rotated alphabetically

STEPS:

1. Meeting room is set up - by Leader
2. Check for quorum (Majority present)
3. Review minutes from last meeting
4. Add any further agenda items as appropriate
5. Arrange the agenda in order of priority
6. Proceed through the agenda (status report as assignments)
7. Recap the meeting
8. Set agenda for next meeting (time, date, place)
9. Critique

Figure 3-6

Rotational Leadership

Leaders don't serve for life, rather, leadership is rotated, giving members an opportunity to hone leadership skills. Rotational leadership fosters full participation and gives each team member an opportunity to experience the rewards and challenges of leadership. It is indispensable to the empowerment process. However, there *will* be individuals who cannot lead.

Likewise, members take turns as recording secretary. In the formative stages, the facilitator will monitor the rotation of responsibilities to ensure that all participate. Initially, roles will be assigned on a voluntary basis. As members become familiar with the process, a regular rotation schedule can be worked out.

Consensus

Groups make decisions by consensus. Doing so requires that sufficient time be spent early in the process to elicit all views and enlist everyone's support. To build trust among the members, gain their commitment, and empower them to assume non-traditional roles, they all must have a voice in decisions.

In the beginning, the facilitator will monitor this process to assure that everyone's view is heard. This will free management to participate fully as members without having to watchdog the process. As the group becomes more experienced, the roles of leader and facilitator are assumed by those within the group. Later, as members become more comfortable, they will "run the show" themselves.

Of course, groups don't arrive at decisions in a vacuum, and they require direction, particularly in the formative stages. *It is essential that management commit itself to giving them this necessary direction.* It is no less essential that management include the members in important decisions that affect them. Members will object strongly if they are "left out of the loop."

Problem Solving

Group problem solving is not new with High Performance Work which makes use of tools that have been utilized for years. Among the most useful of these is *brainstorming*, which builds on the breadth of experience and knowledge represented by the members, and figures centrally in their self-actualization.

The Fishbone Diagram, another time-tested quality tool (see Figure 3-7), can be extremely helpful in rooting out the underlying causes of problems. Pareto analysis is useful in quantifying the magnitude of the problem as an aid to effectively sequencing an action plan (see Figure 3-8). This example, from an on-going group, demonstrates that quantifying issues provides valuable real data for discussion. There remain numerous quality tools to aid in tracking and solving customer-based issues. (See Chapter 10 for additional information regarding the use of these tools.)

HIGH PERFORMANCE WORK SYSTEMS ROLES AND RESPONSIBILITIES

Traditional job descriptions are used to set pay levels and minimum job requirements. But in many cases, very little of the job is actually performed. *Here's why*: The description is normally written by a human resources professional after reviewing the job duties with the supervisor. The employee who actually does the job invariably has little or no input, and, as skills improve, the job description becomes outdated.

In the world of High Performance Work *competencies and skills* descriptions become more useful than traditional job descriptions in identifying the flexible roles of group members.

Competencies/Job Skills

Having the group define the competencies and skills needed to perform roles in the organization is more effective since the group will modify roles as conditions and requirements change. Flexibility is introduced so that cross-training is feasible. The introduction of competencies and

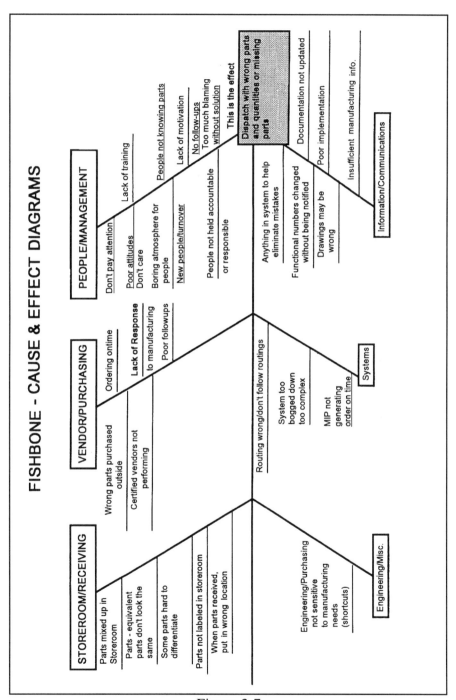

Figure 3-7

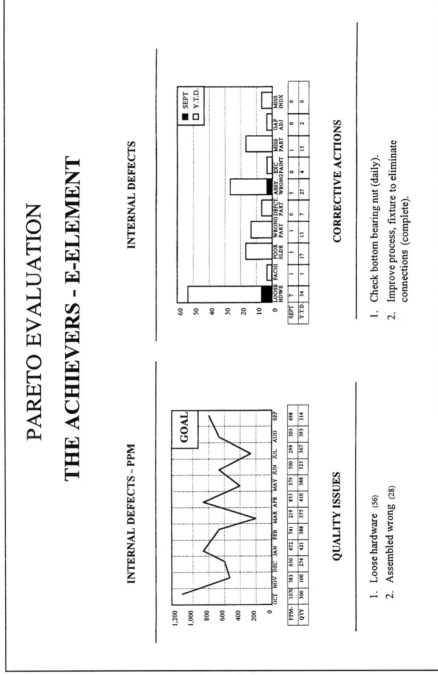

Figure 3-8

skills descriptions paves the way for alternative wage payment systems. This important area is discussed in more detail in Chapter 5.

Communications

Communication often breaks down when information is passed through several "layers" in an organization. In a High Performance environment, members communicate person-to-person; there is no need to use the management as a go-between. Since communication is so central to the High Performance approach, members must carefully develop communications and listening skills. Management must re-think what it communicates and why. The focus of communication must be to provide all data needed for successful decision-making.

Problem Solving

Unlike the traditional environment where problem solving is delegated to professionals and management, in a High Performance organization problem solving is an important role of multifunctional work groups. High Performance thinking recognizes that all personnel are innovative problem solvers.

Member Selection

High Performance Groups, once empowered, take a great interest in their own performance and in that of the business—and feel a special responsibility to achieve excellence. It isn't just a job to them—it's a mission. Therefore, it is small wonder when they begin to take an active part in recruiting, interviewing and hiring new members. In many cases, the new hire must receive the team's blessing as well as management's. This veto power fosters a sense of ownership among the members.

Peer Evaluation

As members assume responsibility for the selection of new hires, they must also assume a role in evaluating each other. In the beginning, they may do this through input to management. Later, as management "drops back" to become coach and boundary manager, peer evaluations may be conducted directly by the team, with input from management. This later stage *must not be rushed* and only comes about once trust among the team members has been established.

Forming Functional Teams

Traditional organizations are most often managed functionally. Often, initially the High Performance organization is formed along these lines. It is possible to effect dramatic improvements in the department's operating efficiency and productivity without getting overly involved with other departments.

At first, when such linkages are necessary, supervision will serve as the emissary. As empowerment grows, the members themselves will take on the linkage roles. This contributes to improved problem solving and allows results to be communicated to both internal and external suppliers.

Eventually, the group will be able to look at parts of the process not directly under its control and make improvements in the flow from one area to another. This will give rise to cross-functional thinking that consolidates processes and eliminates sequential operations.

Forming Cross-functional Groups

It is harder to train cross-functional groups (i.e., those from distinct and separate organizations/departments or functions) and harder for them to achieve high performance. However, when they're successful, the pay-off can greatly exceed that of a single-function group since an entire business process (from supplier to customer) can be improved.

Cross-functional concepts support initiatives around "design for manufacturability," "co-engineering," and project management programs since the process is applicable to all of these organizations. Customer focus becomes both an internal and external emphasis with detailed planning throughout all functions and improved interdepartmental communications.

HIGH PERFORMANCE WORK SYSTEMS JOINT MANAGEMENT/LABOR EFFORT

If unions are part of the system, their commitment to, and support of, HPWS concepts is important. *Trust* is imperative to any relationship and certainly key in an organized environment. Potential benefits in a union setting which need to be clearly articulated include:

* Support for union leadership

* Improved worker health and safety

* Reduced grievances/issues

* Pre-notification of changes

* Access to more and better information

* Fewer misunderstandings—perceived management mistakes

* Higher visibility—looking after members' best interests

* Better public relations

* Improved resolution handling

* Increased attendance at meetings—more membership support

* Strengthened industry economic position

* Increased employee satisfaction

* Better worker education and training

- Reduced job stress

- Less unnecessary supervision

- Improved interpersonal relations

- *Trust* will be enhanced

Summary

A High Performance Work System is only as successful as the work groups and support systems that comprise it. Success, in turn, is shaped by a broad range of factors. Careful structuring and sizing of groups is essential. In addition, members must strategically undergo some formal training across a range of interpersonal and problem-solving skills. They must learn how to plan and schedule work, make decisions by consensus, interface with other teams, deal with conflict, and measure their results. The unequivocal support and commitment of management and of the unions (when they are a presence) is essential.

By taking pains to incorporate the key ingredients of success into their HPWS and HPWS-like initiatives, many companies have achieved remarkable results. Their stories are the subject of Chapter 4 and serve as a catalyst towards HPWS.

Chapter 4

HIGH PERFORMANCE OPPORTUNITIES

> *"The wicked leader is he who people despise.*
> *The good leader is he who the people revere.*
> *The great leader is he who inspires the people to say,*
> *'We did it ourselves.'"*
> *—Chinese philosopher Lao-Tsu*

The case for implementing High Performance Work in any organization is a powerful one. This innovative approach to work management and accomplishment promises a rich array of benefits and opportunities no other system can match.

If ever there was an idea whose time is <u>now</u>, HPWS is it. Downsizing, re-engineering, and break-through thinking have brutalized the work force. For many it's now or ...

Drawing on the experience of several companies, this chapter illustrates why HPWS makes such compelling sense for companies today. And, it provides solid data for building a "business case" for HPWS.

HIGHLIGHTS: **The Dynamics of Change**: As they struggle to cope with the dynamics of change and meet the challenges it poses, many U.S. companies are implementing High Performance Work Systems.

The Proof Is in the Results: Does HPWS really work? Companies that have tried it report results that are nothing short of remarkable. Several are showcased here.

Tapping Employees' Potential: High Performance Work Systems have been shown to unleash the full intellectual and creative potential of employees far more consistently than conventional work systems.

High Performance Opportunities: Many companies have grown into organizations of vast breadth and diversity. High Performance Work Systems, as the human dimension of Total Quality Management and Time-Based Management, can help organizations forge the common bond they need to move *beyond survival* in the coming years.

THE DYNAMICS OF CHANGE

"The order is rapidly fadin
And the first one now
Will later be last
For the times they are a-changin'."
—Bob Dylan

These are turbulent times for organizations. Change is everywhere. New marketplace demands, global competition, accelerating technology, increasing regulation, environmental concerns, demographic shifts among workers and consumers, the need to balance job and family responsibilities—these forces and others have obliged us to rethink some of our most cherished assumptions about work and productivity.

There is pressure to do more and more with less and less—and do it better and faster.

In their struggle to cope with the dynamics of change and meet its challenges, many companies are exploring high involvement approaches in one form or another. As noted theorist, MIT professor and author Peter M. Senge writes, "In an increasingly dynamic, interdependent, and unpredictable world, it is simply no longer possible for anyone to figure it all out at the top. The old model, 'the top thinks and the local acts' has given way to integrated thinking and acting at all levels."

Admittedly, only a small percentage of workplaces, according to the U.S. Department of Labor, can be said to operate totally in a High-Performance mode. But, by all accounts, virtually every major corporation is at least experimenting with the concept.

Many of those companies who have switched to High Performance Systems report dramatic results. Westinghouse Furniture Systems boosted productivity by 74% in three years through work teams; Lake Superior Paper Industries turned an anticipated $17 million loss into a $3 million profit following the introduction of a high-involvement work system. Such companies are best-positioned to cope successfully with the ongoing dynamics of change.

The responses of other companies span a continuum from tightening their control mechanisms to dipping their toes in the water of organizational re-design, with many in-between teetering on the diving board.

Most current organizational theorists agree it's only a matter of time before every success-driven major company will make the move to high-involvement work systems. Granted, it's not the kind of move any company makes casually. Putting a High Performance System in place and getting it to work demands a sizable investment. Management must commit wholeheartedly to the concept and be prepared to openly communicate its game plans and objectives to the work force.

HPWS will be a prerequisite for moving *beyond survival* into sustained growth and prosperity into the next century. If anyone should view survival as a right, Senge reminds us that fully one-third of the Fortune 500 industries listed in 1970 vanished within thirteen years. The objective then, is to do what it takes to move beyond survival!

THE PROOF IS IN THE RESULTS

Word is getting out: HPWS really works. As more and more companies recast themselves in the High Performance mode, their achievements are getting increasing play in the business press.

To make a case for High Performance Work Systems, one need not search far for some very convincing examples of success. They're being showcased everywhere.

Consider this: Corning's specialty cellular ceramics plant brought defect rates down from 1,800 parts per million to 9 through new work systems. In Minnesota, Dana Corporation's valve plant trimmed customer lead time from six months to six weeks. Procter & Gamble's work team plants are 30-40% more productive than non-team plants. Miller Brewing Company outperformed the U.S. brewing industry for six consecutive years and increased market share by 6% through team-based plants.

In all fairness, these organizational redesign initiatives are often accompanied by investments in technology upgrades and expansions; therefore, High Performance Groups can't be given *all* the credit for these eye-opening improvements. But, they are clearly a central factor, and theorists accord much of the credit to what they call socio-technical re-design, or the harmonious fusion between technical and social work systems.

What goes into a High Performance success story?

Leadership is one element, and leadership begins with management. Management must lead the way, supporting the process at every stage. Management must also put its money where its mouth is. Organization/people redesigns demand a major commitment of energy, time, and money. But, no other investment promises such rich dividends.

On the next few pages appear case histories of several companies, representing a broad spectrum of industries, that have benefited from High Performance-type Work Systems. No two companies are alike, but they all share an unshakable commitment to excellence and an unwavering focus on the customer:

Item: After one Eastman Kodak manufacturing unit in Rochester, New York, adopted the HPWS approach in the late 1980s and early 1990s, team members began to introduce measurements, including financial data, that helped them view their work unit as if it were an independent business. Said one, "The question we [constantly] asked ourselves was, 'If this were my business, what would I do?' It really began to feel like it was our own."

Today, the organization has three fewer layers of management than it did in the late 1980s. Moreover, the unit reported:

- Overall product conformance to specifications improved 27%;
- Statistical process control variance improved 228%;
- Output increased 12%;
- Costs reduced 11%;
- Uptime increased 2%;
- Safety increased 67%.

Item: In an industry already pushed beyond capacity, General Motors invested nearly $2 billion to introduce a totally new automotive concept and open a manufacturing facility for it in Tennessee. Today, GM's Saturn family of cars is an industry leader in customer satisfaction and group profit per dealer. Sales continue to grow and the plant is adding personnel to meet demand.

Behind this success is an extraordinary partnership forged between labor and management. With guidance from both the UAW and Saturn's management, self-managed work teams of 8-15 people function in a consensus, decision-making mode to select their own members, design their own jobs, and manage such team activities as material control, incidental maintenance, scheduling, record keeping, budgets, and resource needs. Manufacturing work teams are serviced and supported by resource teams and all are expected to devote significant time to training.

"The team-based consensus process is Saturn's lifeblood, with decisions balancing technology, people, and business needs," says Marty Storm, a former Saturn executive and a member of its original study team. "Driven by an innovative risk-reward system, continued success at Saturn is rooted in its core values of commitment to customer satisfaction, a determination to excel, teamwork, trust, respect for the individual, and continuous improvement."

Item: From 1989-1993 Pitney Bowes reduced its call centers from 99 to 7. During 1994 a thorough analysis by a cross functional/cross organizational group totally re-evaluated organizational design, competencies, career pathing and compensation strategies.

During 1995 this process will result in further changes and refinement. "We thought we were really creative until we asked our people to help us plan the future—everyday we learn something new," said Patti Davies, director of Business Operations, Central Division, for Pitney Bowes.

Item: Between 1988 and the early 1990s, following a major socio-technical redesign that created a plant-wide infrastructure of self-directed work teams, Chevron's Rock Springs, Wyoming, chemical plant reported:

- A 48% productivity improvement;
- A 21% decrease in operating expense;
- A 18% increase in production;
- A 15% labor cost reduction.

Item: GE Capital made the switch to a team-based operation at its Charlotte, North Carolina, and Danbury, Connecticut, Credit Centers in the late 1980s. Customer dissatisfaction with their quality of service had provided the "impetus" for the change. Figures 4-1 and 4-2 show the results of the switch to team-based operations.

Item: At Asea Brown Bovery (ABB) Relays, self-directed, customer-focused teams have:

- shortened product cycles from 16-18 weeks to 2-4 weeks;
- improved on-time shipment from 78% to 100%;
- redesigned products to improve manufacturability with engineering type tests conducted by the manufacturing team;
- reduced total project cycles from 26-32 weeks to 16-18 weeks while improving documentation and customer satisfaction.

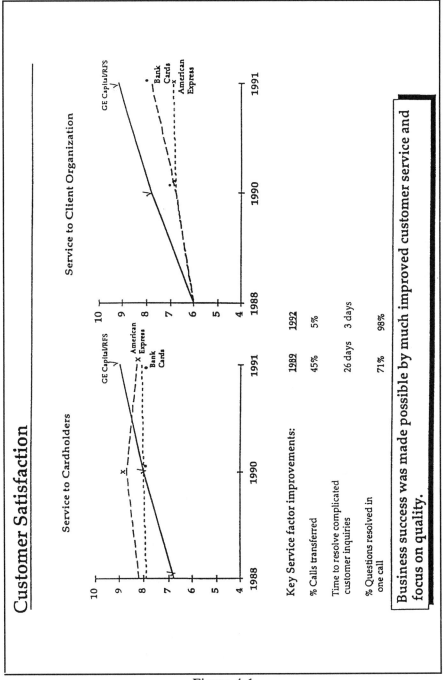

Figure 4-1

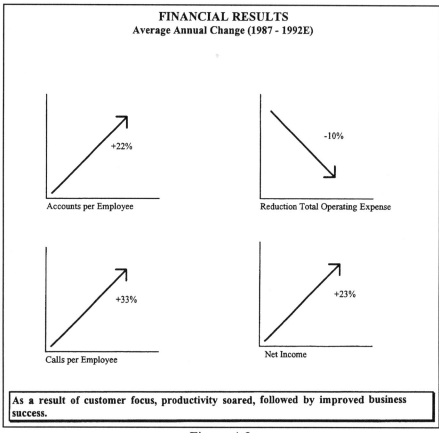

Figure 4-2

Item: Globe Metalurgical Inc. became the first small company to win the prestigious Malcolm Baldrige National Quality Award.

Before winning the award, Globe had been just another aging, rust belt supplier of commodity metals, staying alive on the strength of sales to the ailing steel industry. It has become the leading source for specialty metals to the chemical and foundry industries worldwide. Behind this remarkable transformation was a management-led leveraged buy-out, a strong R&D focus, a high-value-added niche marketing strategy, and the introduction of flexible work teams.

Item: Committed to maintaining growth levels and returns that rank among the top 10% of major U.S. corporations, General Mills is implementing a range of strategies to boost productivity companywide. These include encouragement of innovation and speed of execution; introduction of state-of-the-art equipment in plants and mills; focused partnerships with suppliers; and finding better ways to mesh people and technology through High Performance Work Systems. Over the past five years, General Mills in Cedar Rapids, Iowa, has reported:

- A 30% increase in output per labor hour;
- A 100% increase in production;
- Only a 40% rise in total head count.

"Their independence was almost total," stated Plant Manager Bill Mowery on the work teams. "No bossing was required."

At the General Mills South Chicago plant, per-case labor costs have been reduced by 38%, and 30-40% improvements in cost savings and speed of execution are likely. "High Performance Work Systems involve new ways of doing things," stated former Plant Manager Colin Christie. "We're finding that people are highly motivated to reach their highest potential and improve General Mills' competitive advantage."

Item: Shenandoah Life Insurance Company introduced self-managed teams in 1990. "Previously, we used an assembly line approach, with work passing from one department to the next," stated Jack Cochran, Assistant Vice President of Customer Service. Typically, each employee performed a single, highly specialized task along the way. "Absence at one station could cripple the line," he says.

No longer. After the changeover, the typical time for processing a policy dropped from 27 days to *one,* and costs decreased as well. "I used to own a few narrow tasks," reported one clerk. "Now I own the customers I serve through the life of their policies."

During one five to seven year period:

- Total transaction volume increased 38%;
- Individual work output increased 65%;
- Average service time spent on each policy decreased by 37%;
- Streamlined teams (reduced from 33 to 22 members) saved $250,000 a year.

Shenandoah Life was so overwhelmed with requests from companies wanting to see their revised work operations that they started charging money for a tour. Moreover, the University of California began studying the company in an effort to anticipate college curriculum needs of the future.

Item: When Jack Stack and 118 others bought the Springfield Remanufacturing Corporation from International Harvester in 1983 for $9 million, they were able to raise only $100,000 in equity. With a debt-to-equity ratio of 89-to-one, they couldn't afford to make even a $10,000 mistake.

That was then. In 1991, Springfield Remanufacturing reported annual sales of $70 million and had a work force of 650 (up from 119). The value of a share of Springfield stock in those eight years rose—from a dime to $18.20!

They did it, in part, by creating an environment of total trust and open-book management. "The biggest barrier is ignorance of business," says Stack. "Most people think that profit is a dirty word.... They have no idea that more than 40% of business profits go toward taxes. They've never heard of retained earnings. They can't conceive how a company may be earning a profit and yet have no cash to pay its bills, or how it might be generating cash and yet operate at a loss. That's the kind of ignorance that you have to eliminate if you want people working together as a team."

Stack instituted a massive business education process for all employees, teaching them the rudiments of business, how to keep score, and how their actions impact the balance sheet. He also gave them ongoing access to company financial information.

Item: After years of commitment, hard work, and experimentation, Union Carbide in 1995 created an almost leaderless plant in Hahnville, Louisiana. Group members were selected through a peer process and all were trained in numerous management techniques (interpersonal skills, leadership, etc.).

Having being involved in "kicking off" this new approach, the author and the plant management feel confident the resulting structure and developmental focus will result in "the facility operating significantly below normal operating costs."

Item: In the mid-1980s, Tusca, Arizona-based Magma Copper Company looked back on a 25-year history of adversarial industrial relations. "We had made it an art-form," recalls union leader Don Shelton. Bitter strikes in 1967, 1971, 1974, 1977, and 1980 had almost destroyed the company. In the late 1980s, management and labor agreed there had to be a better way.

A work-system re-design was instituted, leading to the implementation of self-directed work teams throughout the company. Operating in a newfound spirit of trust and open communication, management and labor co-authored a Statement of Principles and Philosophy which became the modus operandi for implementing the new system. They signed an unprecedented 15-year labor contract, introducing gain-sharing for all employees.

Item: After moving to self-managed teams, the Aid Association for Lutherans Insurance Company boosted productivity by 10%, cut case processing time by 75%, and eliminated 150 positions through attrition and early retirement. "The skills and abilities of many workers were underutilized, and jobs tended to be boring because of their narrow scope," recalls Jerry Laubenstein,

Vice President of Insurance Product Services. "Decisions were being made away from the problems to be solved, and that affected both the timeliness and the quality of our service." He adds, "If we didn't have teams, we would need 100 - 150 more people today."

Item: At GE, a revolution known as "Work-Out" has dramatically changed the way things happen. "Layers insulate," writes Chairman Jack Welch in an annual report. "They slow things down. Leaders in highly layered organizations are like people who wear several sweaters outside on a freezing winter's day. They remain warm and comfortable but are blissfully ignorant of the realities of their environment."

At GE's Lynn, Massachusetts, plant, it took 30 weeks to make product in 1987. By 1993, with work teams on the job, it took four! At the Schenectady, New York, turbine plant, unsupervised teams of hourly workers run millions of dollars worth of milling machines that they specify, test, and approve for purchase. The cycle time for the operation has dropped dramatically.

"It is embarrassing," says Welch, "that .. we've been dictating equipment needs and managing people who knew how to do things much better and faster than we did."

TAPPING EMPLOYEES' POTENTIAL

As is evident in the previous real-life examples, the case for High Performance Work Systems is a powerful one, representing as it does the indispensable human dimension of Total Quality Management. Put simply, *without High Performance, TQM doesn't work as well.*

Business magazines and journals abound with stories of almost super-human achievement and commitment that result when workers are given the training, confidence, and support so central to the High Performance philosophy. As former Citibank CEO Walter Wriston writes, "*The person who figures out how to harness the collective genius of the people in his or her organization is going to blow the competition away.*"

Evidently, there's still a lot of collective genius going unharnessed. According to research from the Publishers Agenda Foundation:

- Nearly one-half of the work force (44%) say they do not put a great deal of effort into their jobs over and above what is required.

- Fewer than one in four workers (23%) say they are performing to their full capacity.

- Three-quarters of the work force (75%) feel that management does not know how to motivate workers.

- Nearly three-quarters of the work force (73%) feel that workers get the same raise regardless of how hard they work.

- Two-thirds (67%) feel that workers today want more of a challenge on the job.

- Over two-thirds (68%) say that people don't see the end result of their work.

High Performance Work Systems can help change all that. They offer immense opportunities to tap the dormant energy and potential of the work force and create a real competitive advantage.

That's not to say it is easy. The system is sound, but making it work takes vision, persistence, and more than a little courage. If Total Quality Management won't work without High Performance, High Performance won't fully work without management leadership, constant training, and a single-minded focus on the consumer.

Everyone in the organization must adopt new approaches to work to make this journey. Senior management's role is to establish a vision, policy, and goals, and to provide the **direction** and **resources** to achieve them. Management establishes standards and plans and acquires the requisite interpersonal and technical skills; their role is to create a healthy work environment. Competencies in management should include team building, setting standards, coaching, and organizational knowledge.

Individuals must seek to continually build not only their technical capabilities but their interpersonal skills as well in order to deal productively with their co-workers.

HIGH PERFORMANCE OPPORTUNITIES

"In the beginner's mind there are many possibilities; in the expert's mind there are few.
—Zen philosopher Shunryu Suzuki

Most organizations are under tremendous pressure and are challenged to generate service and profits at unprecedented levels. Most want diversity, total quality and results to create worth. Ironically, today's work force is a gathering of separate individuals in search of a common purpose. High Performance Work Systems, as the human dimension of Total Quality, can provide both a much-needed "bond" and the means to realize potential.

Make no mistake: HPWS is no quick fix. The investment required to install it, drive it forward, and keep it on track will be substantial.

We're talking surgery here, not Band-Aids!

But, if the payoff only approaches what other HPWS companies have achieved, it will be the best investment ever made. Working in groups bound by a common purpose, and equipped with the information and autonomy they need to do the job, employees will feel a new sense of ownership in their work and its outcome. As a result:

• Products and service will be brought to market faster and more economically than ever before. The whole industrial chain, from drawings to marketplace, will flow far more smoothly.

- Productivity will soar and quality improve as newly empowered employees take a more personal interest in reducing costs, shortening cycle times, cutting organizational bureaucracy, and serving the customer.

- Innovation will become the norm—at every level.

- Given the direction to build partnerships with customers and suppliers—and the resources to fulfill that mandate—employees will strengthen their relationships with both.

- A new pride in the organization will result, manifesting itself both within the workplace and throughout the community. Employees again will feel responsible for the organization's success.

Increasingly more and more organizations are showcasing HPWS results. This activity and interest level puts real teeth in the argument that High Performance Work Systems will become standard operating procedure for government, industry in general, and customers in particular.

It suggests that the sooner and more fully HPWS is implemented, the more prosperous the future. High Performance Work Systems are not a total answer in themselves. Many system issues and processes also require work. However, organizations which sit out the HPWS revolution are likely to find themselves noncompetitive.

Summary

In the 1990s, a bewildering range of trends—demographic, political, technological, environmental, and market-driven—has obliged many companies to rethink some of their most cherished assumptions about organizational structure and work methodologies. Many organizations are recognizing the need to put greater decision-making power and information in the hands of the people who do the work.

Invariably, this thinking leads to High Performance Work Systems. As the human dimension of Total Quality Management, HPWS unleashes the full potential of employees in a whole new way. As many organizations across a broad spectrum of industries have discovered, HPWS makes possible high levels of profitability and customer satisfaction. As demonstrated by the examples provided here, whether in the late 1980s or in the 1990s and beyond, HPWS works!

The objective of Chapters 1-4 of this book has been to build awareness and understanding of High Performance Work Systems and what they can accomplish. With Chapter 5, we begin to look at the *action steps* needed to implement HPWS.

Chapter 5

ANALYZING THE PRESENT WORK SYSTEM

> *"Before one can know where he is going*
> *He must first know where he is. "*
> *—Burmese proverb*

Every revolution has to start somewhere. In the transition to High Performance Work Systems, the starting point is a careful analysis of the current work system and organizational structures.

Through a gap analysis, workers and management can lay out the steps to redesigning and improving existing work systems and, ultimately, achieving the vision of a High Performance Work System. This chapter suggests how that analysis might best be conducted.

HIGHLIGHTS: As a first step, get the employees in the system involved. Interview them regarding their likes, dislikes, ideas, etc.

Organize teams to flow chart the current work systems, all the way from supplier deliveries through delivery to customers (both internal and external).

Use the data gathered thus far to draw a clear picture of the existing technical system and its needs. (Note, the re-engineering phenomenon is not discussed here, but, an understanding of the actual work process flow is beneficial to HPWS implementation.)

Next, *zero in on the social system*—the attitudes, group processes, interactions, and behaviors of the people who make up the work system.

Pinpoint and describe current deficiencies and conduct a "gap analysis"—an examination of the current work system versus what a High Performance redesign would look like.

Develop and implement ideas for changing the work system and closing the gaps utilizing focused benchmarking.

CONTENT:

Today, most organizations are home to a bewildering array of work systems. For the manufacture of high-volume repetitive products, for example, continuous processing is the norm. More project-oriented operations employ a range of approaches from manual processes to computer-aided project management. (Many of these operations are organized functionally across a range of products and services.)

Large "turnkey" operations, meanwhile, tend to be run on a project basis with reduced emphasis on the functional organization. And a few organizations, principally in manufacturing and recently in the service sector, have begun to rely on broad-based, cross-functional work groups. In fact, this approach is being adopted in white-collar areas with measurable success.

Today, the business environment in which we work is, by necessity, in constant flux. For that reason, it is essential to have good tools for analyzing and updating current work systems—or for building new ones entirely—to keep pace with changing needs. To stay competitive, companies must change. They will need to embrace high-involvement work concepts.

In this chapter, there are discussions on a variety
of structures, analysis tools, reward systems, and
job designs. They're intended to help
organizations take a long, hard look at where
they are now—and where they want to go.

CURRENT WORK SYSTEMS
ORGANIZATIONAL TYPES

It is important to clarify to which organizational type your existing work
unit belongs before you can analyze it properly. Work systems currently
in place throughout industry fall into a number of categories.

Functional Organization

Historically, organization by function has been the rule for government
and industry. Relying on scientific work analyses, organizations have
institutionalized divisions of labor, building them into specialties such as
Engineering, Logistics, Production Control, Marketing, Manufacturing,
Finance, etc.

In the past, this specialization was necessary to improve work techniques
and refine procedures. That was when manufacturing was king, and
labor comprised most of the "value added" in the manufacturing process.
That's no longer the case.

Today, the balance has shifted toward the service sector and that factor,
combined with the incredible power of automation, has lessened the
percentage of total cost represented by labor.

Rugged individualism has long been a cherished trait, and, until recently,
few have placed much stock in teamwork at the action levels of the
organization. But functionally organized multi-layer organizations are
under constant attack by more efficient approaches pioneered in the
United States and perfected by the Japanese. The days of that timeworn
approach may be numbered.

Project-based Organization

As the role of labor has diminished, organizations have relied increasingly on expertise concentrated in specialized outside groups. Some entities, especially utilities and process industries, find they can no longer maintain capabilities in core processes and must purchase them from outside suppliers. That's why turnkey operations appear to be cropping up everywhere these days.

Product Line Organization

Not infrequently, organizations are built around specific products which shape sales channels, design capabilities, and manufacturing processes. Many product lines are still supported by a central functional organization for development and tend to be specialized in marketing and manufacturing. These organizations are often used in conjunction with a matrix organization.

Profit Center Organization

Profit center management was created to achieve the benefits of a small organization in a large multifunctional organization. Each function is represented in the profit center, operating somewhat more independently of the central organization than it would with a product-line management approach.

Matrix Organization

Matrix organizations focus on multiple requirements, such as multiple markets, for the same or similar products. This type of organization has become popular among large multinationals. Specific responsibilities are clearly communicated based on customer needs and organization. It makes it possible to maintain communication of customer requirements as well as functional organization for specialized skills. The key issue to manage here is insuring accountability with multiple reporting relationships. Someone must ultimately have at least 51% responsibility for the final decision.

Team Concept Organization

Work teams per se are not a new idea in the United States. Even in organizations that have barely flirted with the High Performance concept, one may find natural work teams moving toward a common objective over an extended time period. They may have a single function or several.

Among the various sub-species are Project Teams, which are formed for a specific purpose, have a limited life span, and are charged with solving a specific problem or delivering a specific product or service. Over the last four decades the Lockheed Corporation has had the "Skunk Works," a project team that created such successful military aircraft as the U-2, SR-71, and the Stealth Fighter.

Project teams tend to use many of the same tools as functional work teams but often lack the advantage of long-term work relationships among members. Quality Circles were project teams with undirected goals. They offered training in problem-solving, communications, and work analysis. But since the Quality Circle was left to devise its own mission and goals, with no guidance from management, results were predictably inconsistent. When the project was completed, the Quality Circle team was broken up and the members returned to their natural work teams.

Teams that work on projects with deliverables to an end customer for profit are known as Customer Focus Teams. They often include one or more representatives of the customer's organization—a factor that greatly enhances communication with the customer. But, care must be exercised to prevent overcommitment by the team.

TOOLS FOR EVALUATING THE CURRENT WORK SYSTEM

Analyzing an existing work system requires the right tools, and the know-how to use them properly, as will be seen on the following pages. Regardless of the job, it's always important to have the right tools. Just ask anyone who has ever tried to tighten a screw with a butter knife.

Fortunately, there is a broad array of tools available for conducting a thorough analysis of the current work system. The tools can be used in combination and are relevant to the social, or behavioral, aspects of the system as well as the technical (tasks, activities, processes, technology, etc.).

Structured Interviews/Focus Groups

An effective way to research and describe the existing work climate is through structured interviews of employees and/or groups at each level. By asking carefully constructed questions, it's possible to gain insights into performance, existing communication, and employee and management effectiveness. Then, by encouraging interviewees to expand on their answers, the interviewer can develop a fuller picture of the situation from the perspective of the line employee and the management team.

Interviews can also provide a window on the "hidden" organizational chart in determining how a business is actually run.

Data Gathering Surveys

Surveys can be helpful if they are carefully tailored to specific conditions. They are significantly more time efficient than one-on-one interviews, a big plus in large organizations. However, surveys don't reflect "nuances" or degrees of feeling, nor do they allow any room for amplification questions. Thus, they should generally be used to supplement interviews.

Operations Analysis

Somewhere in the files of most organizations' archives is a written operations analysis that includes details of the organizational structure and, often, standards and practices. It's worth looking at. But, be aware that most operations analyses have a shorter shelf life than cottage cheese. They tend to go out of date as innovations are installed (especially when management isn't aware of the innovations).

Event Mapping

Event mapping is an outgrowth of the advent of complex management information systems. It's a technique for documenting when new information or material is added to a process.

Event mapping, thus, provides a means of defining core business processes. By specifying who owns which data, it defines organizational structure as well. It is a useful tool for implementing procedural changes, since it establishes local benchmarks and can shed light on duplicate effort and erroneously used information.

Flow or Process Charting

Probably the clearest way to depict a complex process is to draw a flow chart. Its accuracy can then be verified by auditing participants.

Flow or process charting yields more hard facts about the way work tracks than do interviews. It is far more effective than verbal descriptions in helping people visualize a process. Unfortunately, the chief limitation of a flow chart—or event mapping, for that matter—is that it cannot get at the "story behind the story." It reveals nothing about the behavioral and motivational issues involved.

Note: For more information on flow charting, see Chapter 10, "Measurement/Metrics."

ANALYZING CURRENT REWARD SYSTEMS

Rewards differ from recognition in that reward systems are usually focused on tangible, quantifiable results. Recognition normally centers on behavioral change and is more subjective. It's axiomatic that a reward system must reasonably compensate the people doing the work. *Existing reward systems need to be analyzed in light of the "changes" that the employee base is being asked to make.*

Incentive Compensation

Incentive compensation is used widely as a way of rewarding employees at all levels, from the boardroom to the line. Pay is scaled according to how close the employee comes to meeting productivity goals.

Though many companies are using incentive compensation with great success, its biggest flaw is its occasional encouragement of measures that boost volume and streamline production cycles at the expense of quality without regard to customer needs. Unless quality and customer considerations are carefully designed into an incentive system, mediocrity will prevail and customers will flee.

Group Incentives

The aim of group incentives is to foster teamwork. In principle they make sense, but they can be difficult to implement effectively. Reason? Unless individuals are willing to subordinate their own needs to the overall task, they are more likely to compromise on quality than pursue it. Many group incentive systems fail because the group is not clearly defined. When defects slip through, the group gets blamed, and the individual avoids responsibility.

Day Work

Day work compensation is based solely on the time spent working, irrespective of quality or output. Where day work is concerned, the caliber of one's effort is immaterial; showing up is what counts.

Used widely for non-repetitive manufacturing, day work compensation assumes that people will generally work at a reasonable pace, even when they're not paid a premium to do so.

Measured Day Work

This variation on conventional day work incorporates standards for monitoring and evaluating work performance. However, employees are not compensated directly on the basis of their performance but on the overall performance of the company.

The idea behind measured day work is to get everyone focused on the total business process rather than on narrow piecework incentives. But, because the rewards are so detached from individual performance, the motivation provided by this type of system is questionable. Measured day work does de-emphasize piecework standards, but it can require close supervision and control.

Pay for Performance

Traditional performance measures are engineered standards, but pay for performance systems allow for benefits to be derived from the achievement of overall objectives set for an individual and/or a team. These business objectives are usually generic and are progress indicators for a product or a service success. As a concept, pay for performance is a good one, but it can be difficult to implement and manage.

Gain Sharing

The growing popularity of Employee Stock Option Plans (ESOP) and other employee ownership programs has given rise to gain-sharing programs. Gain sharing emphasizes rewarding the team as a whole with a more equal distribution of gains to all employees. Measured, communicated objectives must be achieved for payouts to the group to be activated. The best candidates for gain sharing compensation are dynamic companies that thrive on innovation. Quality tools need to be well established for this system to work with a focus on meeting customer needs.

Pay-for-Skill-and-Knowledge

In a pay-for-skill-and-knowledge system, the more skilled you become, the more you're paid, regardless of whether your skills are directly connected with your current job. That's because pay-for-skill-and-knowledge recognizes that cross-functional training is required to support High Performance teamwork.

This system works best with multi-skilled, flexible work teams—especially in companies experiencing rapid growth or technology breakthroughs. However, it's difficult to design, maintain, and accurately measure.

Caution: Each of these processes has its merits and pitfalls. The key is to design a system that rewards results that support the organization's efforts and goals. A few considerations prior to attempting to change any reward system:

- People must have the tools, processes, and resources to achieve the results desired.

- Customer focus must be a cornerstone.

- That which is *measured and rewarded* will get done.

Competency pay or measuring the value one brings to an entity (normally based on both technical and defined behavioral criteria) is becoming popular in some circles and can be very effective in driving change. However, this approach requires an extensive amount of time, energy, and resources.

JOB DESIGN

Around the turn of the century, industrial engineer Frederick W. Taylor perfected a new, "scientific" approach to job design. It called for dividing work into simple, yet highly specialized tasks, and standardizing the procedures for doing them. Machine pacing was used wherever possible.

Taylor's work design scheme, used with historic success in Henry Ford's first assembly line, has been the dominant approach in industry for decades. It was well-suited to a work force characterized by low levels of education and multiple languages, and to simple manufacturing processes that relied more on hands than minds. Since jobs could be mastered in a few hours, employees were easily replaced—a factor that gave management excessive power over workers until they organized.

While Taylor's system was hailed as a bold leap forward when it was first introduced, organizations eventually saw that simple, repetitive, boring work fails to provide a sense of satisfaction. Inevitably, high levels of absenteeism, turnover, and sloppy work resulted. To motivate workers, extrinsic rewards, such as higher pay and incentive plans, were introduced. The reasoning behind this was that, when there is no internal satisfaction from doing good work, the organization must provide external rewards to motivate individuals.

But ultimately, wages and benefits became very expensive. (Today, some assembly line workers are paid over $25.00 an hour for work that can be learned in less than a day.) Moreover, pay incentive plans often became counterproductive, as employees learned to "beat the system" and earn rewards for doing less work. And, since the work itself did not encourage self-control, legions of managers were needed to ride herd on the workers. Large, cumbersome staffs were also required to design the work system, administer pay-incentive systems, train workers, establish schedules, etc.

In short, Taylor's "scientific management," which reduces work to simple, repetitive, unrewarding tasks, has today become associated with low-motivation levels, reduced quality and productivity, inflated wages, and expensive staffing requirements. It was once the engine that drove U.S. industry, but its relevance and effectiveness have expired.

HIGH PERFORMANCE WORK DESIGN

The purpose of analyzing the existing work system is to set the stage for the organizational HPWS refocus and to give employees and managers the information they need in order to begin regrouping. It takes an in-depth understanding of the social and technical components of the current work system to be able to begin making recommendations for further refinements.

A careful work analysis will yield a sizable body of data, which can be of inestimable help in managing and controlling the operation's process variances. Indeed, the flow charts, operations analysis, and key variances analysis have a range of applications. They:

- Provide a basis for education and training for new team members;

- Facilitate technical problem-solving by teams and individuals;

- Reinforce statistical process control and quality improvement programs;

- Are useful in developing performance measures for the organization, teams, and members.

Once the existing work system has been analyzed and understood, several key issues need to be addressed in redesigning it as a High Performance Work System. These issues reflect employees' needs as well as technical and productivity considerations.

For the *individual member* in a work group it is necessary to:

- Provide an optimum variety of tasks within the job;

- Design each employee's tasks so that he/she perceives them as a meaningful part of the process;

- Regulate the length of the work cycle to maximize skill development and work flow and minimize stress, boredom, and physical demand;

- Ensure that each job assignment includes some of the preparatory and process control tasks.

For the *work group* it is necessary to:

- Build interlocking tasks between work group members. That is, after all, the essence of teamwork. Design the work flow so that interdependent processes are physically near one another;

- Rotate work assignments; no team member should be permanently stuck in a high-stress job;

- Establish control (linkages and influence) over the boundary tasks and support services. (i.e., What are the boundaries?);

- Empower team members by giving them a say in setting quality and quantity standards;

- Make sure the team gets regular, timely feedback on how it's performing against expectations;

- Structure the work to produce a distinct, recognizable outcome;

- Provide training and tools needed to facilitate the process.

Summary

A crucial step in the transition to HPWS is a careful analysis of existing work systems. What category do they fall into? How do they operate? How are employees compensated, rewarded, and recognized for their performance? These questions must be addressed as the work unit prepares to move to HPWS.

To gather the requisite data and conduct a useful analysis, it is important to become knowledgeable in the use and application of a battery of specific evaluation skills, such as interviewing and flow charting.

The next stage of the HPWS journey is to formulate a High Performance vision, making sure it is consistent with the company's overall objectives and expectations. That step is the focus of Chapter 6.

CREATING COMMITMENT TO A
HIGH PERFORMANCE VISION

"Where there is no vision, the people perish."
—Proverbs, 29:17

A High Performance Work System does not exist in a vacuum. Rather, its vision must be clearly and explicitly tied to the company's short-and long-term objectives, commitments, expectations, and values.

The High Performance vision is the subject of this chapter—what goes into it and how to ensure that it keeps the group moving in the same direction as the company.

HIGHLIGHTS:

- Aligning the work group's mission with local and corporate missions

- Goal-setting for a High Performance vision

- Principles in establishing the vision

- Determining desired measurable behaviors

- Evaluation of behaviors and results

THE HIGH PERFORMANCE VISION

As you are undoubtedly aware by now, High Performance Work Systems are about employee empowerment and self-direction, among other things. But they do not offer employees a charter to "do their own thing."

Rather, it is absolutely essential for a High Performance System to move in the same direction as the company's overall mission, goals, and principles. This means the work group must be clear on the letter and spirit of the corporate mission and make sure that its own mission and operations are consistent with it in word and deed.

Conversely, it means that management must commit itself fully and unambivalently to the HPWS and to making it work.

That's an important point. **Too often glaring discrepancies arise between what a company says and what it does**. It extols change, but clings to the status quo. That cannot be permitted to happen. Once buy-in to the High Performance concept happens, management must invest the resources necessary to make it succeed. Management must walk the talk. That point is addressed in more detail later in this chapter.

Mission

The first step in creating a HPWS vision, then, is to make sure it meshes with the long-term goals and mission of the organization. Consider this *sample* of a formal Mission Statement for Newco.

*Newco's mission is to be <u>the **leader**</u> in delivering quality products and services for [   ], and that meet the needs and requirements of our customers and contribute to their success.*

*To ensure customer satisfaction, Newco will provide <u>**value-added integrated solutions**</u> that are driven by superior technology and performance.*

*Newco's <u>**employees are committed to leadership standards**</u> in applying the company's unique combination of expertise and resources to meeting societal goals for sustainable growth.*

Competition is intensifying, technological breakthroughs are becoming harder to achieve, and customers are growing tougher to please. Yet, even in this challenging environment, companies can meet and exceed profitability objectives provided management, employees, and the work organization all pull in the same direction and keep the corporate mission top of mind and at the center of every action.

Goals

To be meaningful, goals must be *specific and concrete*. To be achieved, they must be *measurable and measured*. As organizations strive to create environments of openness and trust—ones that encourage employees to take pride in the organization and responsibility for its success—they must set tangible goals that *hold management accountable*.

A number of tools are available for this purpose, including employee opinion surveys, 360° feedback mechanisms, small focus groups, etc. These tools make it possible to accurately gauge behavioral change—variables like loyalty, trust, and morale—as well as the organization's progress against quality and productivity goals. (See Chapter 10 for more information on measurement.)

Companies must be steadfast in measuring themselves against goals. Most organizations have established at least four.

Here are Newco's:

Customers: *Become an organization that is measured by contributions made to customers' success and satisfaction.*

Shareholders: *Achieve leadership results and competitive advantage in the areas of [   ] through the focus on management of [   ].*

Employees: ***Create an environment of openness and trust in which employees take pride in the organization and feel responsible for its success.***

Community: *Assure positive corporate citizenship by actively contributing to local communities where employees live and work.*

There is no latitude in the requirement that the High Performance Vision lines up with the organization's missions, goals, and principles. It is up to each individual work team to march with the organization, not against it.

Guiding Principles

How goals are achieved is as important as what the goals are. What do you stand for? What will you tolerate? What will you reward? What are the unwritten rules that make your organization and culture what they are?

These questions run through every individual's mind at all levels of the organization. They can be boiled down to a single question: *What are you all about?*

Total Quality Management, Time-Based Management, personal development, teamwork, meaningful recognition and rewards—these are crucial principles in any corporation progressing towards a High Performance Work System (see Figure 6-1). Some guiding principles through which organizations can realize their goals are:

- Partnerships inside the company and with suppliers to serve customers' requirements.

- Time-based management, project management, and customer-focused metrics.

- **Teamwork** and **empowered participation**.

- A safe and environmentally sound workplace.

- **Recognition** and **reward** for excellence.

- Innovative product and service offerings.

- Participation as a good citizen of the community.

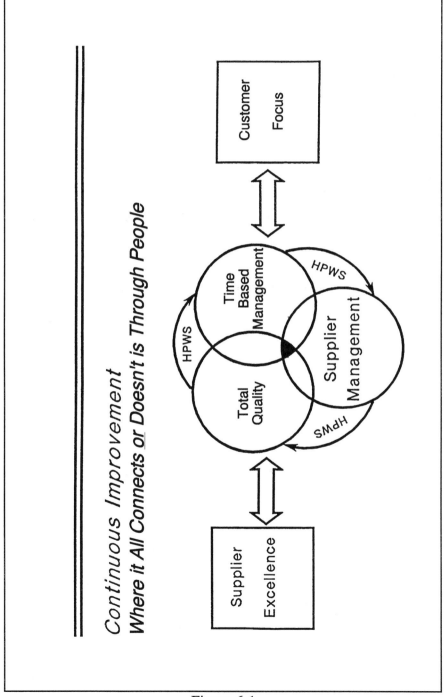

Figure 6-1

DESIRED MEASURABLE BEHAVIORS

Before setting out on a journey, one must know the starting point. Translated into HPWS terms, that means organizations need to take stock of current organizational culture and employee behaviors before mapping the route to HPWS. (For more on how to make the transition, see Chapter 7.)

Getting there requires behavioral changes at every level, from senior management through middle management, line supervisors, and white- and blue-collar employees. Virtue may be its own reward, but don't overlook the value of rewards and incentives in promoting this paradigm shift. *At first, reward behaviors. Later, begin recognizing behavioral change and reward results. In all cases remember, that which gets measured, gets done!*

The following considerations should figure in defining, motivating, and measuring behaviors.

Empowerment

Employees across all roles must develop a mission, describe their job, and establish critical objectives and metrics with which to judge performance. The roles of each employee should mesh like the gears of a Swiss watch. Each must understand his/her role in realizing group objectives.

It is equally important for the group to align its mission with the organizational mission in order to set appropriate objectives, delegate levels of authority, and establish accountability for group results. In so doing, the group can determine what kinds of support it will need from outside resources.

Organization

The group should be structured around its work objectives, not around its members! Organizing around people, rather than work, will undermine the group's effectiveness and keep it from realizing its objectives.

Change Management

Every new movement needs its champions—a cadre of skilled and spirited advocates who make sure the operation gets off the ground and airborne and stays on course. Champions of the HPWS should be identified as early as possible. Their chief role, as agents of change, is to steer the process from one stage to another. *Part teacher, part peacemaker, part evangelist*, they need strong skills in conflict resolution; they need to know how to listen and to motivate; and they must have the authority, energy, and stamina to get things done. To be effective, they require the support of management and the respect of fellow employees.

Employee Evaluation Process (Behavior-based)

A process must be formulated for assessing employees' performances according to selected criteria, such as their ability to work in a team, and their contributions to profitability and customer satisfaction. *Evaluation is everyone's right and responsibility in a High Performance System.* Peer reviews, as well as subordinate reviews of supervisors, team leaders, and managers, give everyone a part in the measurement process.

Buy-in and Commitment

The importance of senior management's support has been a constant refrain in this book. Management must be a champion and not just a supporter. While the value of mission, goals, and principles cannot be overstated, they will ultimately count for little unless the organization wholeheartedly buys into and commits to the program. Without this "buy-in," HPWS will struggle in getting off the ground. The organization will "disconnect" and view it as little more than management "du jour."

To put it bluntly, management must put its efforts where its verbiage is. Financial support, along with operations review inclusion and integrated communications, are the lifeblood of High Performance Work Systems.

Financial and Budgetary Support

It takes training and development in teamwork, group dynamics, presentation skills, and total quality management, among other areas, to make a High Performance initiative succeed. Training doesn't come free, so adequate financial support and budgeting are crucial. However, the expense of development, like other hard costs, can be managed and be cost effective.

Different organizations determine their investment in development according to different formulas—3-5% of sales, 10 days per year/per employee, etc. What's important is that the *company be willing to invest and know what the investment means.*

Operations Review Inclusion

Since High Performance Work Systems figure centrally in day-to-day operations, they should be regularly covered in staff meetings, operational reviews, and management discussions.

Traditional operations reviews tend to focus only on financial and recently-in-progress quality indicators. In HPW, they must also look at the core process of moving the organization to a higher level of effectiveness. By seeing to it that HPWS is placed on agendas, management sends a clear message throughout the organization: This is important enough to be looked at and managed! Operational efficiencies can't help but benefit. Inspection indicates management cares enough to question not only results but the underlying behaviors and processes.

Integrated Communications

Traditional wisdom notwithstanding, silence most emphatically is not golden, at least not where organizational communications are concerned. Once the organization has bought into the HPWS concept, it becomes important to "talk up" the process through the use of every available forum and communication mechanism within the company.

Routine communication tools such as newsletters, roundtable discussions, employee luncheons, and videos can be used to rally support for HPWS, keep everyone current on its progress, and stimulate discussion.

A caveat: Many companies habitually undermine their own best efforts by stinting on internal communications. If there is a rule of thumb, it is this: *when in doubt, over-communicate*. If you're not sure the message has been received, send it again. High Performance Work Systems are an unfamiliar concept to many people; only through a regular program of ongoing communications will management make its commitment and mission understood.

Summary

Without a High Performance Vision, there can be no High Performance Work System. But the vision must be concrete, meaningful, and consistent with the overall corporate vision. Mission, goals, and principles must be clearly articulated and aligned to ensure the vision is more than empty puffery.

True organizational change takes time. Patience is critical and in this case a virtue. Meanwhile, progress must be measured every step of the way, and its strategies carefully aligned with internal and external influences. At the same time, the organization must support the initiative unequivocally—through communications, funding, open discussion, and other means at its disposal.

If these elements are in place, the High Performance Vision can be achieved, as you will see in Chapter 7.

Chapter 7

CREATING A TRANSITION PLAN TO ACHIEVE THE VISION
(3 POINT ALIGNMENT)

> *"Getting there is half the fun."*
> —*Cunard Lines advertisement*

This chapter sets out a step-by-step process for developing a behaviorally-based, measurable growth plan for achieving the High Performance Work System Vision as it was detailed in Chapter 6.

HIGHLIGHTS: While the specifics of the plan will vary by company, the process itself is universally applicable. The ultimate aim of the plan, of course, is to redirect the organization's vast human and technological resources toward building a High Performance organization in every sense of the term.

Having clarified its current behavioral position through the history work role (Chapter 1) and established its long range vision (Chapter 6), the work unit is now prepared to develop a prioritized transition plan for proceeding. (See Figure 7-1.)

Such plans are never simple. It takes a series of steps to achieve a properly developed, long-range vision. The best way to do this is to focus on one step—or destination—at a time, making sure to endow it with measurable characteristics. In order to assure alignment with the long-range vision, the next succeeding step should also be brainstormed, planned and scoped. This process is called the "3-point Alignment Process" and is shown graphically in Figure 7-1.

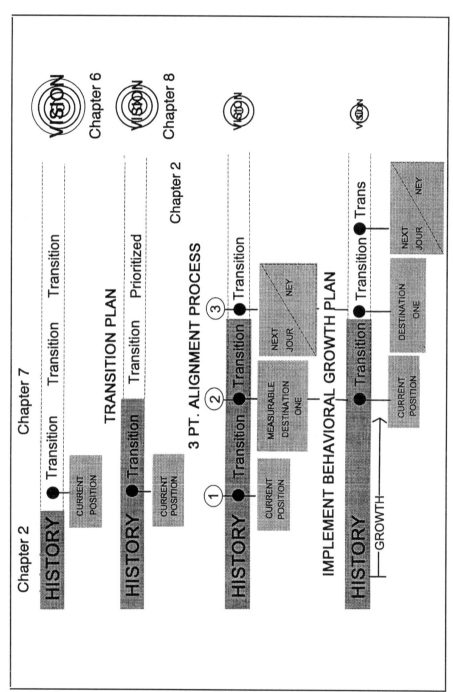

Figure 7-1

SIX STEPS TO BUILDING HIGH PERFORMANCE WORK SYSTEM CAPABILITIES

What methodology does a unit follow for defining Destination One and the behavioral plan to achieve it?

Even if we think we know where we're going, how, in fact, do we get there?

Again, the words of the Chinese philosopher Lao Tzu are relevant: "A journey of a thousand miles must begin with a single step."

The following "graphic" outlines the sequential steps an organization must take to create and implement a simple, yet comprehensive, behavioral-based growth plan leading to a High Performance Work System. This plan becomes the road map for the organization's journey to its final destination.

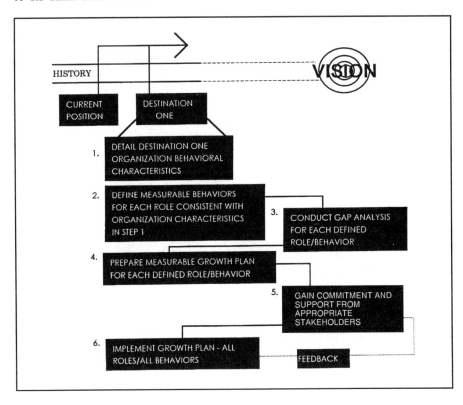

A note on steps one through six: this process depends on a commitment from everyone in the organization to align individual and group behaviors with the organizational characteristics defined for each destination. This process is repeated through as many destinations as required to complete the journey.

Of course, visions often change as they become clearer, and this process might well become one of continuous improvement.

The following examples, comments, and suggestions will help clarify and detail each step of the process:

Step 1: **"Detail the desired destination and organization behavioral characteristics."**

- EXAMPLES: (See Chapter 2)
  - Support the High Performance Work System process

  - Integrate HPWS with other management tools

  - Expand the team's decision-making boundaries

  - In making decisions, consider "people needs" as well as business and technology

  - Eliminate negative symbols

  - Initiate performance-based risk/reward plan

  - Train leaders to be trainers and facilitators

- COMMENTS AND SUGGESTIONS:
  - Be sure that each behavioral characteristic is in direct alignment with the vision as determined in Chapter 6.

  - Be sure that the characteristics align with each other and reflect all functions and roles. All segments of the organization should be covered.

- Once the list of characteristics is complete, it may be helpful to paraphrase them to confirm that nothing has been omitted and that they describe a complete functioning organization.

- Proceed at a consistent pace. It is better to make steady progress than to wait to make a large advance.

- Couch behaviors in a way that allows them to be measured. Make sure that it will be apparent to the individuals and the organization when desired behaviors have been achieved. (See Chapter 10 for more on measurement.)

Step 2: **"Define the expected, measurable <u>behaviors</u> for each organizational function and role consistent with the organization characteristics described in Step 1."**

- Look at the entire system—functions and roles across every category of employee, team, and decision-making body, including exempt, non-exempt, union, non-union, line, staff management, resources, suppliers, customers, positions of authority, leaders, owners, and others.

- All functions and role behaviors should be integrated and mutually supportive. For example:

	FUNCTION/ROLE	BEHAVIOR
Example 1	Individual Worker	Attend and participate in team meetings
	Work Group	Use team processes
	Meeting Leader	Facilitate team meetings
	Department	Provide meeting facilities and resources
	Mid-management	Budget and provide time for meetings
	Senior Management	Sanction the concept

	FUNCTION/ROLE	BEHAVIOR
Example 2	Project Engineer	Learn and apply group problem-solving skills
	Engineering Team	Learn to solve problems as a team
	Engineering Leader	Teach group problem-solving skills and assist the team in problem-solving
	Engineering Dept. Manager	Practice group problem-solving and assist team leaders
	Resources	Join in group problem-solving and provide expertise
	Project Management	Promote group problem-solving and provide the necessary resources
	Unit Management	Encourage and model group problem-solving

- Behaviors should be stated so that they are measurable. (See Chapter 10.)

- Some significant function/role behaviors might revolve around decision-making, problem-solving, customer focus, communication, training, participation, teamwork, contribution, leadership/followership, and the growth process.

Step 3: **"Conduct gap analysis for each defined function/role behavior."**

- Use the result of the analysis conducted in Chapter 5 in addition to the behaviors identified in Step 2 (which will require a broader, more detailed review of the current organizational structure).

- Once you've defined the "gap" between where you are and where you want to be, state it in action terms, i.e., specific quantifiable actions to be taken. This will aid in preparing a detailed growth plan. (See Step 4 below.)

- Because behaviors tend to be closely interconnected, like the gears of a machine, this gap analysis will identify opportunities to positively impact several behaviors with a *single* strategic action. For example, in Step 2, if project management encourages and models group problem-solving, it also opens the door for many other functions and roles to change their behavior. This cascading effect is a useful tool in preparing and implementing a growth plan that deals with cause-and-effect relationships.

Note: as you may see, stakeholder (project) management is crucial here. Discussions, perceptions, fear, disconnects, etc., must be dealt with and handled in a clear manner.

Step 4:   "Prepare   measurable   growth   plan   for   each team/function/role behavior."

- The plan should address what needs to be done by (or for) whom, when it will be accomplished, and how it will be performed.

- Roles must be mutually supportive. Those that are neglected, constrained, or viewed passively by the rest of the organization will lag in their growth toward a High Performance Work System.

- Every function/role should examine its own "bailiwick" for issues to address in support of this growth plan. Among the areas that bear scrutiny are: reward systems (both incentive and equity), boundary management, geography, environment, team development, communications, resistance to change, power and influence, profits, decision-making, facilities, resources, performance, empowerment, accountability, short- and long-term planning, training, and common goals. *Rule of thumb: whenever an issue surfaces, deal with it!*

- The importance of a needs-driven individual training plan will emerge as this process unfolds.

- The same holds true for an efficient communication and stakeholder management system: A growth plan should answer the question, "When does who tell whom about what—and how do they go about it?"

- Another important spin-off of this process is the assistance it provides to designing and implementing performance appraisal systems.

Step 5: **"Gain commitment and support from all roles."**

- As many function/roles as possible should be involved in the process from the beginning, and at every step along the way.

- There should be **no** surprises when it is time to commit.

- It is helpful to ask functions/roles to formally draft their respective plans as well as desired characteristics (Step 1) and expected behaviors (Step 2).

- Once the group is committed, the energy around "make-sense" measurements will increase. (See Chapter 10.)

- Planned performance should be a chief priority of every work team.

Step 6: **"Implement the coordinated growth plans for all teams/functions/roles."**

- Establish a baseline and plan implementation performance measurement process. (See Chapter 10.)

- *Celebrate* achievements; note opportunities to continue growing.

- Throughout the process, **COMMUNICATE, COMMUNICATE, COMMUNICATE**. Seek ideas and comments from everyone in the organization.

- Acknowledge all contributors and engage their help in a smooth implementation.

- Establish effective feedback system for continuous improvement.

Summary

The key to effective 3-Point Alignment is keeping on course as you move from transition to transition. All organizations make changes as they move to HPWS. But many do not "plan ahead" to ensure continuous improvement. The 3-Point Alignment Process provides a tool for planning for continuous improvement.

You *never* get there by design! If the organization is continually redefining its long-term focus and its next journey, it will be pushing toward new behaviors and structures on an on-going basis. This means that there will be constant change which must be examined, evaluated, and, as appropriate, implemented.

As we measure progress by clearly defining "where we are" and what behaviors are expected at "Destination One," the future becomes increasingly clear. Looking beyond this step to the next journey will provide some frank observations regarding change and requirements. If this process is continued over and over, the future becomes less frightening, clearer, and eminently obtainable.

Chapter 8

IMPLEMENTING THE TRANSITION PLAN

> *"It's not so much that we're afraid of change or so in love with the old ways, but it's the place in between we fear... It's like being between trapezes. It's Linus when his blanket is in the dryer. There is nothing to hold on to."*
> —*Marilyn Ferguson, futurist*

This chapter outlines the critical steps for making the transition to High Performance Work Systems and successfully integrating them. And, it provides a model for HPWS implementation at the individual operating level.

HIGHLIGHTS:

- **Transformational Change**: High Performance Work Systems represent big change for most organizations and individuals. Inevitably, many individuals will be uncomfortable with the challenge it poses to the status quo and to systems and protocols they've long set store by. For that reason, strong, resilient leadership commitment will be needed to fully weave HPWS into the cultural fabric of the organization.

- **A Model for Implementation:** Several factors are essential for successful implementation of High Performance Work Systems. Among them: buy-in by management, clear strategy-planning, open communication, the involvement of all stakeholders in work process redesign, and ongoing systemic reinforcement.

- **Perceived Barriers to Success**: Successfully implementing a High Performance Work System is a complex and challenging undertaking that demands a major investment of time, energy, and money. Those embarking upon the journey must recognize this and be willing to pay the fare.

- **The Dynamics of Backsliding and Failure**: The journey isn't over once High Performance Work Systems are beginning to form. Strong leadership, decision-making based on principle not expediency, a well-distributed value system and skill base, and supportive environmental systems will be essential to keep HPWS up and running and to prevent backsliding. *Failures and setbacks will occur*—they are part of growth and the change process.

Transformational Change

Integrating High Performance Work Systems into any organization involves more than mere incremental change in operating style and practices. On the contrary, the change represented by it is nothing short of revolutionary, and its introduction must be viewed, and planned for, in this context.

As stated earlier in the text, conventional management thinking in the western world has many roots in control paradigms introduced by Taylor in the early 1900s. The High Performance Work Systems model is derived from an entirely different paradigm, that of high involvement/commitment.

While management practices have gone through many "flavors of the month" in recent years, proponents of High Performance Work Systems emphasize that this is not a program but a *fundamental change in business style and operation that affects all facets of an organization.* Organizations electing to make this journey can draw an analogy with Cortez burning the boats to demonstrate there was no going back to Europe.

Such transformational change requires vision at the top, not to mention courage and commitment to stay the course—especially as the going gets tough and the surroundings get eerily unfamiliar:

> *"I know that most men, including those at ease with problems of great complexity, can seldom accept even the simplest and most obvious truth if it be such as would oblige them to admit the falsity of conclusions which they have delighted in explaining to colleagues, which they have proudly taught others, and which they have woven, thread by thread, into the fabric of their lives."*
> *—Leo Tolstoy, Russian novelist*

But how does one distinguish between transformational and incremental change? The following comparative model, captures the fundamental challenges inherent in the transition.

ORGANIZATION CHANGE

Incremental	Transformational
• Does not challenge assumptions or values of existing culture	• Attempts to alter the culture
• Modifies or slightly improves the overall operation	• Focuses on significant, breakthrough improvements
• Uses existing structures, procedures, and processes	• Challenges the relevance of existing structures, procedures, and processes
• Minor disruption to "status quo"	• Dramatically alters the "status quo"
• Relatively low risk	• Relatively high risk

Transformational change is clearly what High Performance Work Systems are about. The following are considered essential characteristics of such transformational change:

1. **The need for change must be strongly and widely felt.**

    HPWS offers very real, tangible, competitive advantages to organizations and benefits customers in compelling ways as well. These advantages were described in Chapter 4 (High Performance Opportunities). Nonetheless, the need for change may not be readily apparent to all, and must therefore be clearly and painstakingly communicated to everyone in the organization.

2. **The change must ascend to the top. Leadership actions must dramatically demonstrate commitment.**

    The impetus for change *should, but need not, come from the top*. But, management must embrace it as quickly as possible if the change is to be organization-wide and pervasive. This is not just a matter of clearing barriers from the path of those implementing the change. The fact is, unless those in key decision-making positions are willing to assume risk, there is little chance their subordinates will.

    In times of transformational change, leadership must take actions that demonstrate their commitment in powerful and unmistakable terms. At Tektronix, a vice president decided to share confidential information on the company with everyone in his division. His peers on the Corporate Council called him crazy. "I want to turn this business around," he replied. "I can't do it without them, and they can't do it if they don't know how we're doing." Within a year, his division had made a dramatic turnaround, and the "crazy" VP took satisfaction from seeing some vocal critics following his example.

3. **The perception of early success is critical.**

    The introduction of High Performance Work Systems is no quick fix. In large and complex organizations, transition can take 2-5 years. It is important, therefore, to communicate and celebrate early successes to maintain momentum and to combat resistance.

4. Maintain focus by a *single, grand theme* for the change.

Don't overlook the importance of a succinct but clearly articulated theme for change and keeping everyone focused on it. If it truly captures the spirit of the purpose of change, it can go a long way toward illuminating the best paths and choices. Consider the Ford Motor Company's guiding theme, "Quality is Job 1," Disneyworld's "Making People Happy," or The Ritz Carlton's "Ladies and gentlemen serving ladies and gentlemen." For these organizations, their themes are powerful shaping forces in their strategies, plans, and actions.

5. There must be widespread, highly visible dispersal of information relating to the change.

Communicate. Communicate. Communicate. Management must overcome the antiquated notion that information is a perk of power. It isn't just a question of giving people the information they need to do their jobs, but one of generating trust through openness.

And as important as trust is, *what* is shared is crucial. Financial data, customer data and process information all focus on bottom line impact. Just ask the folks at Tektronix. Moreover, inaccurate or insufficient information breeds mistrust. Consider the words of the ancient Greek poet Theognis of Megara: "He who mistrusts most should be trusted least."

6. There must be a clear description of a possible future that challenges and motivates.

Vision is often considered an over-used leadership maxim. But unless the organization has a clear and consistent view of where it's headed and the values and principles critical to everyday decision-making, then commitment to change is unlikely. *Management must articulate its vision in crystal-clear terms, making sure that its **behavior reflects that vision** in every way.*

7.   **The change must be integrated into the cultural fabric of the organization.**

High Performance Work Systems can impact all facets of business operations. Consequently, organizations need to review the infrastructure to ensure compatibility. This includes financial systems, human resources policies and procedures, reward and recognition systems, trappings of status, divisive differentiators, etc.

Silos and barriers must come down, and be replaced by boundaries of operation that allow individuals freedom to act. But this freedom is not a blank check: Actions must be guided by the organization's values and principles.

A Model for Implementation

If an organization is to succeed in bringing about the transformational change HPWS requires, the clear and consistently applied commitment of management is essential. Every study of successful implementation processes supports this contention.

Given the size, diversity, and organizational architecture, the full implementation of High Performance Work Systems throughout an organization will be an exciting process. The graphic below demonstrates four simultaneous drivers in implementation over time:

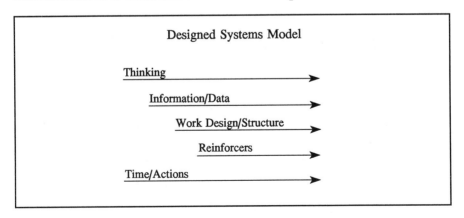

Designed Systems Model

Thinking

Information/Data

Work Design/Structure

Reinforcers

Time/Actions

Thinking refers to the organization's leaders and the way they perceive their roles. By their very thinking, assumptions, and actions, they send powerful messages throughout the organization. So, the change must be consistent with their thinking, and be substantiated by behavior. For those accustomed to the control model of management, this will require a bold mental and behavioral leap.

The way **information** is distributed must change! To re-orient the company along high-involvement lines, employees must have access to information that enables them to understand the state of the business and to do their jobs more effectively. Information channels, traditionally the exclusive preserve of management, must open to everyone in the organization.

Historically, information has moved through organizations like an elevator: information going up, decisions coming down. Information must go to the point where direct action can be taken. Management must "surrender" the power that information has traditionally provided and avoid the paternalistic attitude that bad news will demoralize employees. This new paradigm suggests the end of "day care" and the reinstatement of all employees as adults. If employees are expected to behave as partners in the enterprise, they must be treated as partners.

The third step in the model relates to changes in the way **work** is actually **designed** and performed. Using support functions as resources, work groups now become directly responsible for decisions relating to the design of work and its continuous improvement. "Given some minimal guidance," writes Marvin Weisbord, author of *Productive Workplaces—Organizing and Managing for Dignity, Meaning, and Community*, "most work groups produce designs 85% to 90% congruent with the best that outside experts can produce, and with vastly more commitment to implementing them."

The fourth step is changing the way rewards and other forms of **reinforcement** are allocated. The new reward system must strengthen the changes instituted in the previous steps. Training is aimed at preparing employees to assume and successfully carry out expanded responsibilities.

Corning employees spend 20% of their time in training. At Monsanto Fiber Operations, it's 20% - 25%. At Tektronix, about 15%. "Without adequate training," says William Musselwhite, "you can't make the transition."

Formal compensation systems are, arguably, the most difficult processes to change. Many companies use gain sharing, but the complexities of rewarding individuals and teams without conflict of interest make this a difficult system to implement efficiently and equitably. Pay-for-knowledge or pay-for-skills pose challenges in measurement and application. Books on reward systems abound; *the key is effective measurement and perceived fairness in implementation.*

IMPLEMENTING HIGH INVOLVEMENT WORK SYSTEMS

The following model provides a useful and simple framework for considering the implementation of High Performance Work Systems.

I.   Management Thinking

- Gain management commitment to the change effort
- Explore current control biases
- Explore the commitment as an alternative approach
- Understand implications of change on the management role and the need for personal change
- Develop a clear vision of how the future organization will look

II.   Develop a Strategy

Determine the most appropriate implementation strategy for the organization

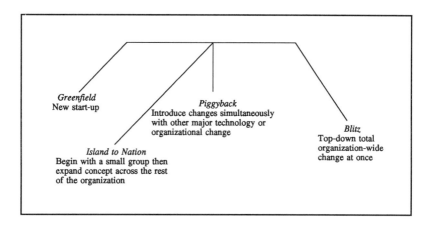

III.   Utilize Lead Systems

Information
Get information to the point closest to where value is being added to the product or service

Work Design
Achieve a joint optimization of the social and technical systems

Reinforcement
Create a reinforcement pattern that assures the change will be institutionalized

Implementation processes usually require the creation of a Design Team or a Steering Committee, as well as the active participation of all stakeholders in the work redesign effort. Many companies retain an experienced consultant, more to act as process facilitator than as an external expert. There *is no cookbook* recipe for implementing a High Performance Work System—*just many essential ingredients.*

Perceived Barriers to Success

Successfully implementing a High Performance Work System is a complex and challenging undertaking. It demands a major commitment and widespread recognition that the flight may be occasionally bumpy.

Among the perceived obstacles are:

- Training costs will go up.

- Middle management may resist change.

- Staff support groups may resist change.

- Workers' expectations for personal growth and development may go unmet.

- Interpersonal conflict may occur (particularly in the early stages).

- Team meetings take time and may slow down decision making.

- Without the union's open collaboration, initiatives can be frustrated. Bargaining needs to be very decentralized to allow parties the room to work things out at the local level.

- Salary costs will go up (particularly through knowledge/skill-based/competency pay for performance systems).

- Seniority and other traditional forms of jobs classification can get in the way unless they're handled with openness and flexibility.

- There may be increased turnover, as people who can't make their peace with the new operating style leave.

Given these potential stumbling blocks, some theorists suggest that companies can expect a performance drop in the early phases of HPWS implementation. Other theorists, with which the author agrees, maintain that such a view can be a self-fulfilling prophecy. To succeed and improve, *expect* to succeed and improve!

The Dynamics of Backsliding

Once High Performance Work Systems have achieved a foothold in an organization, there are numerous forces that may attempt to knock them loose. This *is particularly likely when a change of leadership occurs,* or when the company faces a major business test.

At Weyerhaeuser, several months into their change process, the business took a downturn and they faced a major financial issue. Management's first impulse was to revert to such tried-and-true management methods as freezes and travel bans. But, they took a deep breath, asked the organization to come up with solutions, (which they did!) and the change process didn't miss a beat.

There is less chance of backsliding when:

- Strong leaders throughout the system are deeply committed to a vision of the future.

- Required values and skills for high performance are broadly disseminated throughout the organization.

- Each test of organizational resolve is managed by principle, not mere expediency.

- Environmental support is cultivated through skillful, sensitive interaction.

Summary

As mentioned, there is no cookie-cutter implementation model for High Performance Work Systems. In deciding whether they're ready and willing to embark upon this journey, groups must recognize that:

- The process represents transformational change.

- Leadership commitment must be paramount and highly visible.

- Though implementation may take 2-5 years, *the process never ends*.

- A focus theme should be developed to provide identity and continuity.

- Open communication is essential at every phase.

- A clear vision must be held up for all to see.

- Infrastructure must be adapted to support the change process.

- Actions should be governed by principle, not expediency.

- Work design should involve the participation of all stakeholders.

- Implementation strategies should be customized to the environment and planned carefully.

- Barriers to success need to be faced and overcome.

- Boundaries of operation should be established, and individuals and teams given the freedom to act within them.

- Investment in development should not be underestimated and must be continuous.

- Resistance and discomfort will occur, at all levels, and need to be sensitively and appropriately managed.

As previously stated, once it is implemented, a High Performance Work System is guided by a long-term vision. Keeping the organization on course as it progresses toward that vision is the subject of Chapter 9.

Note: In the attachments which follow, Tables 1 and 2 suggest transition roles for the Design Team, the Steering Team, Consultants, and Organization Members. Tables 3 and 4 provide an example of the criteria and process undertaken by Corning in these areas.

MANAGING TRANSFORMATIONS

FOR THE ORGANIZATION:	FOR TEAMS:
1. From control to commitment 2. From managerial direction to self-regulation 3. From "rugged individualism" to collaboration 4. From narrow tasks to multiple, broad skills 5. From low risk philosophy to high innovation	1. From start-up "Adventure" stage... 2. through Dependence... 3. through Counter-dependence 4. through Resolution... S. through Inflation... 6. through Disenchantment... 7. to Interdependence
FOR INDIVIDUALS:	**FOR ALL SYSTEMS:**
1. From mistrust to trust 2. From doubt to autonomy 3. From guilt to initiative 4. From inferiority to industry 5. From role-confusion to self-identity 6. From isolation to intimacy 7. From self-absorption to generativity 8. From despair to integrity	1. From forces technology to high tech/high tough 2. From national economy to world 3. From short-term to long-term 4. From centralization to decentralization 5. From institutional help to self-help 6. From representative democracy to participatory democracy 7. From hierarchies to networking 8. From either/or to multiple options

Table 1

From Erickson, Walton, Trist, Neisbitt & others
The STS Design Handbook
©1987, 1991 STS Publishing, 132 N. Lafayette, South Bend IN 46601

TRANSITION ROLES

DESIGN TEAM	STEERING TEAM
1. Design own ground rules 2. Conduct or delegate all analysis and design tasks 3. Refrain from over-specification: do not design others' jobs for them 4. Maintain open communication with all parties 5. Make final decision on design	1. Define organizational mission 2. Define project scope, constraints 3. Design the transitional system: roles, objectives, resources 4. Provide sanction, support, protection 5. Evaluate, contribute to design proposals
CONSULTANTS	ORGANIZATION MEMBERS
1. Provide training, information, theory, experience 2. Refrain from "experts' solutions" 3. Be available for frequent and/or lengthy periods 4. Adhere to the principles of "co-learning:" all participants hold special expertise	1. Learn the concepts 2. Contribute ideas 3. Provide critiques 4. Help ensure results

Table 2

By T.D. Christman
The STS Design Handbook
©1987, 1991 STS Publishing, 132 N. Lafayette, South Bend IN 46601

PLAN FOR IMPLEMENTATION

Implementation plans are developed which address moving the work groups toward increasing levels of self-management, developing success criteria and measures, addressing resource requirements, determining skill development needs for all employees, and outlining the changes needed for support systems.

Key Elements

- Determine who is responsible for an implementation plan
- Develop project plan with milestones (short-and long-term)
  - Define change requirements for technical systems
  - Define change requirements for social systems
  - Document and secure needed resources
- Define needed skills to support the design
- Determine training and development requirements and develop plan
  - Technical/social/business
  - Units/team/individual
  - All payrolls

- Assure specific implementation plans are made regarding supporting systems
  - Certification, compensation systems, selection, job configuration, developing internal expertise, career development & planning accounting, information systems, communications
- Define and align success criteria and measures with the work design
  - Propose recommended adjustments to Goalsharing plan based on implementation
  - Assure teams have goals
  - Identify leadership behavior required to support the change
- Develop plan for continuous improvement
  - Assure teams have goals
  - Identify leadership behavior required to support the change
- Develop plan for continuous improvement

Questions Critical for Success

Do you have acceptance and buy-in from the workforce? Leadership? Other key stakeholders?

Have you identified milestones and accountability for the plan?

Are you allowing sufficient time for implementation?

Do employees have the basic skills to maximize other training?

Are resources in place and people trained to provide ongoing coaching and support?

Does the environment support the transfer of responsibility and authority?

Is there a system in place measuring ongoing team performance and providing feedback?

Do teams understand the measures and how to impact them?

How is leadership behavior supporting the change?

Have you linked with engineering support and other technical change efforts?

CORNING

Table 3

IMPLEMENTATION

Changes in work process, equipment, and people utilization take place including changing supporting systems, providing training and development, and determining methods of performance feedback.

Key Elements

- Communicate improvement plans/ redesign and success criteria to all key stakeholders

- Implement improvement in work process, equipment, and people utilization

- Implement changes required in supporting systems

- Customize and further detail of the improvements/design by each work team

- Provide training and development at all levels
  - Basic skills
  - Technical skills
  - Team and social skills
  - Business skills
  - Leadership/facilitator

- Facilitate the transition of increasing responsibility and authority

- Jointly establish and communicate goals and measures (unit, team, individual)

- Determine methods of performance feedback and track

- Recognize and reward, as appropriate

Questions Critical for Success

Have you reviewed your implementation plan and priorities with your business leadership?

Have you identified key competencies for social, technical; and business skills?

How will you handle the gap between current skills and needed skills?

Is your training and certification system ready to support your plan?

How will you handle the need for additional resources and time required during implementations?

Are your measures compatible with business plant, and Goalsharing objectives? Do the teams understand the goals and measures and how to impact them?

CORNING

Table 4

Chapter 9

PROGRESSING TOWARD THE VISION

> *"The art of progress is to preserve order amid change
> and to preserve change amid order."*
> —*Alfred North Whitehead*

This chapter focuses on those aspects of the organization for which continuous improvement will be essential in order to move toward and ultimately achieve the High Performance System Vision.

If the organization is to post continuous improvement in all dimensions, everyone in the organization must understand and support essential organization imperatives. And they must be empowered and encouraged to bring genuine initiative and creativity to bear in moving the organization toward its vision.

Moving Toward the Vision

In an organization geared for High Performance:

•   The organization vision should serve as the foundation for all legitimate improvement goals and activities. If not, something is seriously wrong with either the vision or the goals, and careful rethinking is needed.

•   All members of the organization understand, support, and commit themselves to the organization mission *and know how they fit it*. Organization roles and responsibilities are defined and understood by all. Members must be flexible and sensitive to any changing requirements of the business.

•   Technical, interpersonal, and group process skills are developed to stimulate effective interactions between all individuals and groups.

- Management and staff members model participation and involvement behaviors and processes empowering individuals and groups to function with responsible initiative.

- Mechanisms for solving technical and social system problems and identifying opportunities for improvement result in innovations, goal setting, and action planning.

Measures are identified, charted, and used to monitor trends and gauge progress against goals. The measures provide timely feedback to any member or group so they can evaluate and track their own performance. (See Chapter 10.)

1. The course of improvement follows the 3-point alignment approach to focusing on the organization's vision.

2. The organization's current state relative to each dimension is assessed, answering the question, "How are we doing?

3. The short-term goals for each organization dimension milepost—the definable and measurable next step—are set.

4. The organization's progress is tracked at each milepost to ensure that it is on course and moving toward the vision.

Getting the most out of organization systems

To achieve maximum continuous improvement, each of the following organization systems, influencing member behavior and actions, should be regularly monitored, assessed, managed, measured, and adapted to change. Each is important in its own right and as a part of the whole. If one falters, the organization may suffer:

- The social (people) system
  - Roles and responsibilities
  - Interpersonal and group process skills and knowledge
  - Relationships/supportive behaviors

- Personnel policies and procedures
- Communications
- Measures of performance
- Recognition and reward

- The organization transformation support system

  - Sponsorship
  - Transformation champions
  - Development
  - Facilitation
  - Communication
  - Measures (transformation plan and process)
  - Recognition and reward

- The technical system

  - Technology/processes
  - Equipment and tools
  - Practices and procedures
  - Technical skills and knowledge
  - Information systems
  - Performance measurement systems

- The supplier system (internal and external)

  - Communications and linkages
  - Certification
  - Participation/involvement
  - Measures of performance
  - Recognition and reward

- The customer system (internal and external)

  - Communications and linkages
  - Participation/involvement
  - Service and support
  - Measures of performance
  - Recognition and reward

Summary

Once a High Performance Work System is in place, it will continue to evolve and require ongoing support from everyone in the organization. By its very nature, HPWS is flexible and responsive to change, and progress toward the HPWS Vision depends on continuous feedback and verification that all elements in the process are in alignment.

Detailed, accurate monitoring and evaluation of progress is critical at every step of the way. Chapter 10 describes the various measurement tools available for this purpose and how to use them.

Chapter 10

MEASUREMENT/METRICS

> *There is nothing that is not capable of being measured. At a Haverhill, Massachusetts, hospital in 1907, Dr. Duncan MacDougall placed the beds of dying patients on scales and carefully recorded the weight loss at the exact moment of death. He had succeeded, it appeared, in weighing the human soul.*
>
> —*Momentum* magazine

Having begun to operate in a High Performance mode, how does an organization gauge how far it has come and how much it has changed? What are the standards of measurement for assessing and analyzing change in individual and group behaviors? This chapter discusses tools for designing, applying, and interpreting measurement systems to the High Performance Work System process.

HIGHLIGHTS:

- Reasons for measurement

- Assumptions of behavior-based HPWS

- Steps in measuring team behaviors

- Assessment techniques

- Considerations in selection of instruments

- Procedures for gathering information

- Summarizing and presenting data

- Team metrics

CONTENT: This chapter clarifies why it's important to measure change in the first place, and describes which tools are best suited to specific circumstances and purposes. It also offers guidance on how to decide what kind of data is needed, how to select the right measurement system, and what factors to consider when analyzing, summarizing, and interpreting behavioral change.

REASONS FOR MEASUREMENT

It can be argued that progress without measurement is not progress at all. Unless we know how far we've come, there is no way of assessing how much further we have to go to achieve objectives.

Beyond that, there are several other compelling reasons for measurement:

- To provide comparisons: Measurement provides useful before-and-after comparisons of group and individual behaviors. For example, if no improvement is noted after training, the process may need to be reassessed. Measurements also yield useful comparisons between two or more different procedures. It is important to decide on measures early in the process to increase the likelihood of ultimate success.

- To facilitate communications: Measurement insists on definition. When specific numbers are assigned to data, a common understanding is possible in interpreting a scale or an average. Hard facts clarify performance.

- To ensure objectivity: When specific criteria are used, there is less chance for intuition and biases to distort the evaluation process.

- To track progress: The collection and evaluation of data over a period of time makes it possible to track progress, or its lack.

- To make projections: Depending on the stability of what we are measuring and the presence of forces beyond our control, measurement enables us to predict results and likely trends.

- To verify attainment of goals: Has the group met its objectives? If not, why not? Do the objectives need to be rethought—or does the group need to modify its work systems? Measurement systems help document progress against objectives.

- To provide feedback and reinforcement: For process change and communication. Special data provides an excellent vehicle around which to create a dialogue (pro or con).

- To identify and resolve problems: Quantifying problems makes it easier to focus on them clearly, and to resolve them more efficiently.

- To be part of a closed loop system: Ongoing measurement, communication, and feedback propel the organization. For measurement to have real value, it must be fed back to and acted upon by those being measured.

TECHNIQUES USED IN MEASUREMENT OF BEHAVIOR

Having agreed that measurement is important, the tools and techniques to be used must be determined. The techniques for measuring group and individual behavioral changes and their results fall into two broad categories: standardized and self-designed, each with its own advantages, drawbacks, and applications:

Standardized instruments include a broad array of personality scales, value inventories, and behavioral profiles that can generally be used effectively with large populations and over long periods of time. They fulfill the need to generate a common "language" and an appreciation of the differences in values and attitudes of people.

Advantages
- Don't need to be developed—only administered
- Can communicate with others that have given or taken the assessment and get their reaction
- Can be used with large or small groups

Disadvantages
- Require specialists both to administer and to interpret results
- Format may create "test anxiety" in some people

When Used
- As a starting point for discussing behaviors, values, and attitudes
- When it's not practical or possible to custom-design measurement instruments to the specific needs of the group

When Not Used
- If the group to be measured is very different in terms of age, location, education, etc., from the population for which the instrument was originally developed
- If the reading level of the person or group being measured is low

Self-designed instruments are those that are designed, created, and implemented to conduct a specific measurement. Some self-designed instruments have a one-time only application; others may be adapted for widespread use and thus assume a place in the repertoire of standardized instruments. Self-designed instruments are used for observation, interviewing, and surveying.

Personal Observation: **Examination and analysis of behaviors either directly or indirectly**

Advantages
- Low-cost
- Easy to implement
- Yields information immediately

Disadvantages
- May yield incomplete data since the observer cannot see everything
- An observer's own biases may distort the interpretation
- Knowing they are being observed, individuals may behave differently, thus invalidating the data

When Used
- To assess an isolated incident when broader-based information is not needed
- To verify physical results that cannot be easily interpreted

When Not Used
- When it is necessary to document attitudes, beliefs, or values

Interview: **The use of a person (usually trained or professional) to elicit more detailed and comprehensive responses than those possible from a forced-choice format**

Advantages
- Has a more "personal" touch than a standardized written assessment
- Gives the interviewee more latitude in expressing himself/herself

Disadvantages
- The validity of the results is tied directly to the interviewer's skills. A poor interviewer could antagonize the interviewee or lead him/her into the answers, resulting in false, slanted, or incomplete data
- Takes time
- Can be costly
- It may be difficult to record, interpret, and classify data on the basis of a few interviews

When Used
- When only a small number of people need to be contacted

When Not Used
- When "yes or no" answers will suffice

Survey: **A set of statements or questions, usually written, that generally require only a "yes or no" answer**

Advantages
- Scores can be machine-tabulated to save time
- Confidentiality can be maintained
- A single survey can be used for several groups
- Offers tremendous flexibility: can be used to measure multiple issues and behaviors or just one

Disadvantages
- Format may encourage respondents to hurry through the questions without thinking them through just to get finished
- If overused, surveys may create a "just a number" feeling among employees

When Used
- When specific information is needed from large numbers of people at one or several locations
- When it is necessary to document change over time, since survey can be re-administered

When Not Used
- When the group being measured is too small to justify the cost of developing and implementing a survey
- When the issues cannot be put in clear, concise language understandable to anyone taking the survey

Analysis of existing reports and data

Advantages
- Can be done by one person or a small group, as long as standard measurements and guidelines are adhered to and the interpretations are bias-free

Disadvantages
- Analysis may not reflect unusual or extenuating circumstances that prevailed when the data was originally compiled
- Conditions may have changed since the data was collected, rendering it irrelevant

When Used
- When information is needed quickly
- When comparisons are needed

When Not Used
- When reports are incomplete
- When reports are inaccurate

What to consider when selecting standardized and/or self-designed instruments

Just as you would not use a bathroom scale to weigh steel, you'll want to choose the measurement tool appropriate for the job. A number of factors should figure in your selection:

Preparation
- How much time do you need to design the instrument?
- How much time do you *have?*
- How many people are available? How skilled and knowledgeable are they?
- What other resources can you rely on, such as previous assessments and existing research facilities?

Administration
- Who can administer it? Can the group members do it themselves or will a professional psychologist be needed?
- Is there time to administer it properly?
- Are any special preparations necessary at the test site?

Compiling the Data
- Will the data be machine or hand-tabulated?

- How much training will be needed to compile and summarize the data properly?
- Does it lend itself to clear summarization?

Applying the Data

- Is a correlation (relationship) needed between two groups or time periods?
- Are the responses only to be classified or categorized?
- Is it necessary to itemize each person's response?
- Would a range of behaviors be sufficient?
- Is an "average" (mean) needed?
- Will this survey, etc., be compared to previous ones?
- Does data need to be expressed in terms of standard deviation?

PROCEDURES FOR GATHERING INFORMATION

To yield useful data, it is essential that tools be designed and administered correctly. Some guidelines:

Observations:

- <u>Direct</u>: The observer should be careful to observe only, and not interfere with either the subject or environment. To provide as complete a picture as possible, it is helpful to refer to a checklist with specific items to look for. Several observations may be necessary before sufficient data is yielded.

- <u>Indirect</u>: Indirect observations place the subject in an artificial environment and require him/her to "act out" a response. These include:
    - Role-play, in which the individual dramatizes how he/she would handle a given situation.
    - Reaction, in which the subject's response to a situation depicted on a video or in writing is observed.

Note: An entire group can observe and give feedback. The procedure is not limited to a single observer.

Interviews

- <u>Structured</u>: The format follows a predetermined set of questions or statements on specific topics, allowing room for varying degrees of elaboration by the team member. The most highly structured interview would be basically an oral questionnaire.

- <u>Unstructured</u>: This approach relies less on predetermined questions and more on nondirective and in-depth discourse. Unstructured interviews can often generate more detail than a written report, but they are very subjective and can be influenced by the behavior and interpretation of the interviewee and interviewer.

Surveys

- <u>Opinion surveys</u> usually seek replies to specific questions, which may or may not be related. For example, respondents may be asked their views on pay rates, cafeteria prices, or working conditions in the same survey. Each individual's answers are tabulated separately.

- <u>Attitude scale</u> surveys yield data on the direction and intensity of attitudes toward a company, a policy, a group of people, etc. (More than one attitude or behavior may be measured, but each will be derived from several statements.) Rather than force respondents to answer "yes" or "no," this procedure asks them to choose a numbered response from 1-5, ranging from "strongly agree" to "strongly disagree" for each statement.

Perhaps the best tool or indicator—and very valid reason to move to HPWS—is the bottom line! Keep it in front of *everyone!*

Following are examples of assessment formats which can be adapted and utilized for any organization. Metrics, rewards, and consequences can be directly tied to their application.

HIGH PERFORMANCE EFFECTIVENESS REVIEW
- A Self-assessment -

Section 1: Planning

	Low		Medium		High
	1	2	3	4	5
Does the organization:					
Construct mission statements which clearly define purpose and require us to be a competitive leader?					
Require that we demonstrate continuous performance improvement?					
Eliminate ambiguity within goals, goal setting, performance assessment, and reward criteria?					
Require plans to address rate of improvement in performance for divisions, markets, projects, functional staff groups, et al?					
Develop realistic, time-based strategic and operational plans?					
Make the people who must do the work responsible for determining how to do the work?					
Ensure that operational and project objectives are consistent with mission and strategic goals?					

Section 2: Organizing and Staffing

	Low		Medium		High
	1	2	3	4	5
Does the organization:					
Establish clear definitions of responsibility, authority, and accountability ?					
Provide clarity in the roles, responsibilities, and relationships required for effective management?					
Empower group members to "drive the car?"					
Identify the key competencies required of management and team members for the successful management of their area?					
Identify individual development needs and develop personalized action plans for improving performance?					
Select the most qualified personnel to fill needs?					
Assign personnel to best utilize capabilities and potential?					
Demonstrate management's commitment to support of and involvement in the High Performance Process?					

Section 3: Directing

	Low		Medium		High
	1	2	3	4	5
Does the organization:					
Provide a professional atmosphere where High Performance standards prevail?					
Stress people-oriented leadership and the importance of personal example?					
Create self-managed groups and empower them to perform?					
Encourage and provide employee development and growth?					
Encourage risk-taking, tolerate failure, demonstrate indignance toward mediocrity, and reward excellence?					
Provide an open climate where people can be themselves?					
Provide opportunities for people to make meaningful contributions?					

Section 4: Communicating

Does the organization:	Low 1	2	Medium 3	4	High 5
Encourage open communications and the sharing of real information?					
Maintain good intra- and inter-organizational communications?					
Keep management and customers informed of key problems (no surprises)?					
Keep employees informed and solicit and use ideas, opinions, and input?					
Establish guidelines for effective meetings and enforce them?					
Establish guidelines for effective presentations and enforce them?					

LEADERSHIP/FOLLOWSHIP SURVEY
- An Organizational Assessment -

	YES	NO

1. Does your organization discuss your individual ____ ____
   performance on a day-to-day basis?

   If not, how often? _____
   _____
   _____

2. Do you get a "pat on the back" for a job well ____ ____
   done?

3. Are shortcomings on an assignment brought to ____ ____
   your attention?
   a.   Timely?
   b.   In what manner? _____
   _____
   _____

4. Does your group and management provide a ____ ____
   businesslike and mature environment for
   stressful discussions?

   If not, explain. _____
   _____
   _____

5. Are you allowed to make key decisions? ____ ____

   If not, explain your feelings. _____
   _____
   _____

6. Is the "environment" conducive to support of ____ ____
   your physical and mental needs to perform
   efficiently?

LEADERSHIP/FOLLOWSHIP SURVEY (CONT.)

	YES	NO

7. Do you consider yourself part of the decision process? ____ ____

   If not, please explain. _____

   _____

   _____

   _____

8. Do you feel the organization and your personal goals have been clearly outlined? ____ ____

   Do you fully understand them? ____ ____

9. Have you been encouraged to develop your capabilities? Have you been exposed to an environment which allows you the opportunity to develop capabilities and new experiences? ____ ____

10. Do you believe you are fairly and equally treated and evaluated? ____ ____

    If not, why? _____

    _____

    _____

    _____

11. Is your supervisor a team player? ____ ____

    Does he/she display trust in you as a member of the team? ____ ____

12. Is your supervisor committed to your success? ____ ____

13. Suggestions for improving your work environment:

_____

_____

_____

_____

_____

_____

_____

_____

_____

_____

_____

_____

GROUP MEMBER INTERVIEW FORMAT

GROUP MEMBER_____

DATE_____

Purpose of interview: Gather data to <u>plan</u> a <u>project</u> to <u>increase</u> <u>teamwork</u> and <u>performance</u> in your area of the organization.

1. What is your current assignment?

    _____
    _____

2. What were your past assignments and jobs?

    _____
    _____
    _____
    _____
    _____

3. What procedures are used to manage work flow?   Quantity?
    Deadlines? (Goals, customer order, etc.)

    _____
    _____
    _____
    _____
    _____

4. What procedures are used to manage quality?

    _____
    _____
    _____
    _____

5. Describe your recent successes.

    _____
    _____
    _____

_____
_____

6.   What teams, if any, are you on?

_____
_____
_____

7.   What teams have you been on in the past?

_____
_____
_____

8.   What are the goals and priorities for your area?

_____
_____
_____

9.   What have been some problems recently?

_____
_____
_____

10.   Describe self-regulating work. Are mission, goals, plans all set
       participatively and in a timely manner? How might a self-
       regulating work group help in your area of responsibility?

_____
_____
_____
_____

11.   General comments?

_____
_____
_____
_____
_____

SUMMARIZING AND PRESENTING HARD DATA

Clearly defined goals, stated in measurable terms, are prerequisites to success for any High Performance efforts. Measurements can help teams determine how much training is needed, and how much progress has been made toward goals. HPWS is supported by Total Quality Management and Total Quality is supported by HPWS—they must both be in place to fully drive any organization toward success.

Metrics have been shown to be not only a reflection of business performance but an important component of it. In particular, prompt assessment of problems through quality measurement instruments, such as a Pareto Analysis, provide the groundwork for effective, group-based solutions. Regardless of what's being measured and which measurement system is chosen, the process will be worthwhile only if there is organizational agreement on how the data is to be presented and used.

Data can be described in terms of:

Central Tendency (a number describing the general location of data)

- Mean - the average score if there are equal intervals between successive values

- Median - the number that divides the distribution in half when the values are in order

- Mode - the most frequently occurring number

Dispersion (how scores scatter or spread out)

- Range - a measure of variability found by subtracting the smallest number from the largest

- Variance - a measure of variability within a sample

Correlation (a measure of the extent to which two variables are related, not necessarily in a cause-and-effect relationship) The magnitude of a correlation can vary from -1.00 to +1.00

Standard Deviation (a unit of measurement or a standard way of describing scores in terms of their relation to the mean)

TEAM MEASUREMENTS/METRICS

From a High Performance perspective, measurement serves two main functions: 1) to quantify behavioral development in order to establish training and organizational needs for the work group; and 2) to gauge the progress made to date toward goals, thus reinforcing confidence.

Both Time-Based Management and Total Quality Management directly support the higher levels of employee involvement that are at the heart of the High Performance concept. Through the measurements associated with Time-Based Management, management has indicated which metrics are most vital to the conduct of business. Total Quality Management equips the High Performance organization with tools for documenting and solving problems and sharpening performance.

Once a group has been formed, team measurements should be instituted as soon as practical to avoid losing valuable performance improvement data. Groups should be encouraged to develop new metrics to fit their individual requirements. Of course, any new measurement standards which are designed should be coordinated with existing ones, although many traditional performance measures—productivity for example—take in such a small piece of the total business picture that they will be useful as references only. *As trust and understanding build, measurement standards will be continually modified and improved.*

Early in the life of a group, it will be desirable to conduct a "gap analysis"—a close look at the relationship between where the team is and where it wants to be. An excellent tool for that purpose is the Force-Field Analysis, described on Pages 137 and 138.

Figure 10-1 shows some criteria that are good examples of measures that support teamwork and quality processes. There are numerous tools available to measure a team's performance against goals. Several of these are illustrated on the following pages.

---

* # 7 UP Metrics

- Field Quality
- On-Time Delivery
- Cycle-Time Reduction
- Internal Process Quality
- Supplier On-Time Delivery (Passing Quality Metrics)
- Supplier Cycle Time
- Customer Satisfaction Measurement

Adapted from Baldrige Criteria

Figure 10-1

Cycle time or throughput time is the most effective measurement relevant to High Performance teams. Cycle time measurements can be readily applied to almost all types of work, from information processing to manufacturing. Figures 10-2A and 10-2B depict measurements taken from charts created by High Performance groups in both manufacturing and white collar areas, respectively.

A reduction in delays and rework—with its concomitant shortening of cycle time—usually results from improvements. Process improvement examined at each step may lead to quality compromises at individual steps, particularly if emphasis is placed on meeting engineered standards for a particular operation. One study conducted demonstrated that people were working on a product or the information to support the product only 7% of the total lead time, while assembly and test operations were operating at over 90% efficiency based on "time standards." After focusing the team on appropriate metrics, an 87% reduction in cycle time was achieved.

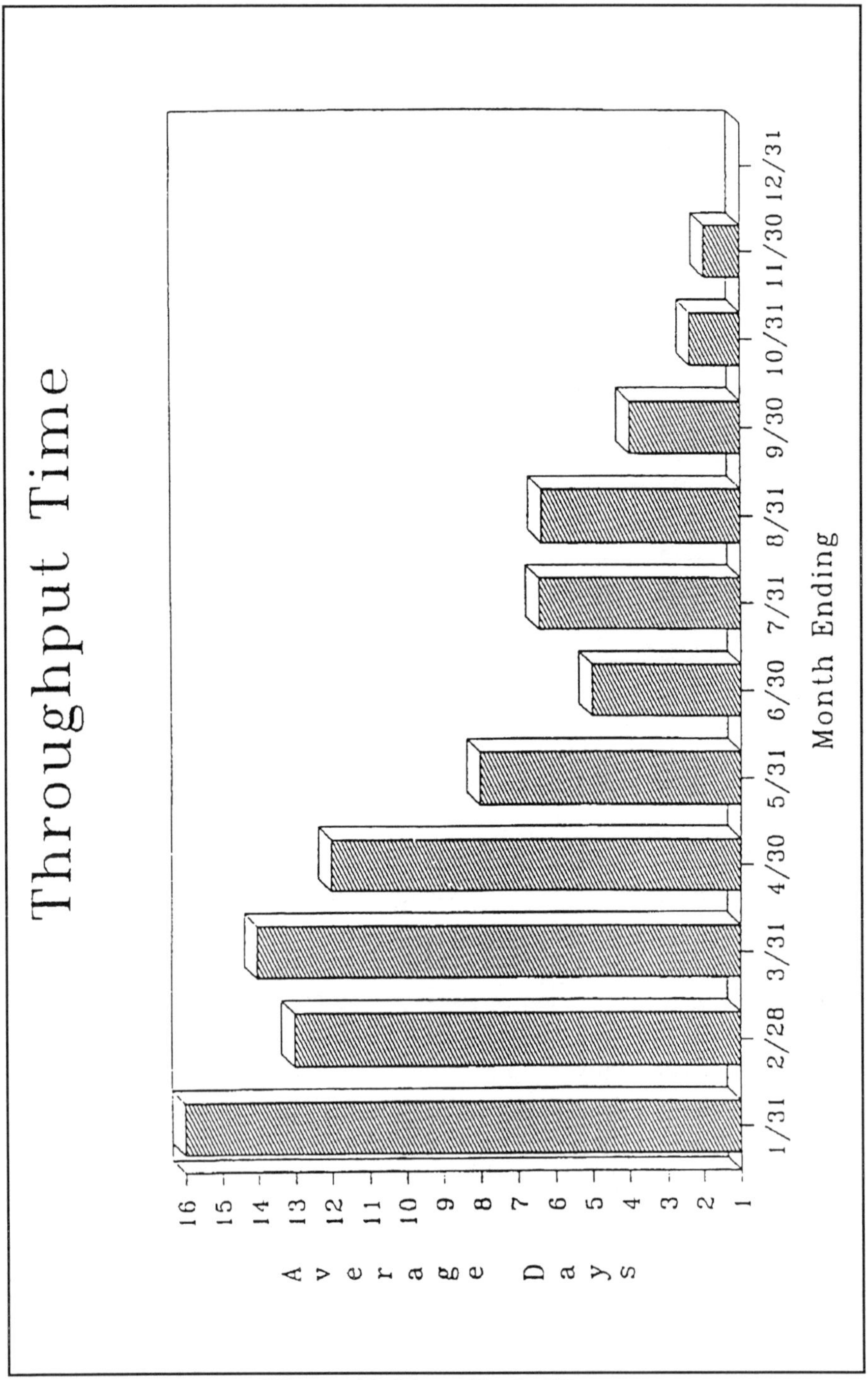

Figure 10-2A.   Cycle Time

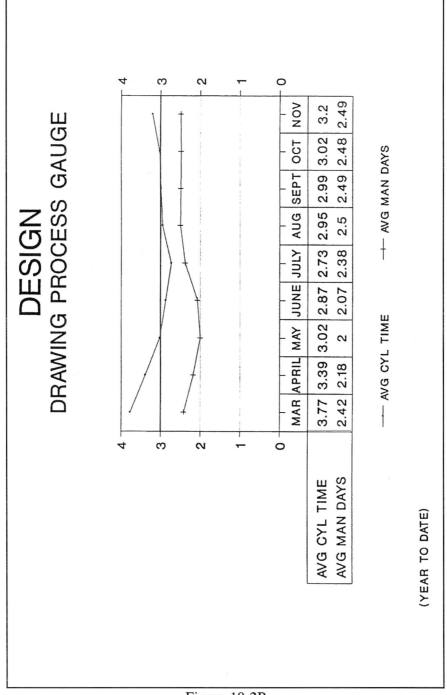

DESIGN
DRAWING PROCESS GAUGE

	MAR APRIL	MAY	JUNE	JULY	AUG	SEPT	OCT	NOV
AVG CYL TIME	3.77	3.39	3.02	2.87	2.73	2.95	2.99	3.02	3.2
AVG MAN DAYS	2.42	2.18	2	2.07	2.38	2.5	2.49	2.48	2.49

—— AVG CYL TIME   ─+─ AVG MAN DAYS

(YEAR TO DATE)

Figure 10-2B

Quality measurement must be integrated into process measures. Timely feedback of defects or problems must be expanded into a frequency analysis, usually a Pareto diagram, which then becomes the basis for a root cause analysis and action plan. These "work" level measurements are usually different from the measurements used by management but are supportive of financial improvement.

Delivery of actions according to plan is also a powerful measure for all teams. This may be demonstrated by an on-time shipment chart (Figure 10-3A), or may be in the form of a process map, Gantt chart, or similar project follow tool (Figure 10-3B). A Gantt chart is also useful for developing a transition model that allows a group to visualize a path to the vision and set priorities for the initial destinations. As the 3-Point Alignment Process develops intermediate benchmarks and additional data, the plan is continuously refined and alternatives are developed, increasing buy-in and success.

As groups mature, they normally learn process development techniques. Unfortunately, all too often process development techniques are imparted without the individual or group understanding their ability to impact the metric. This lack of understanding often causes the organization to incorrectly view the Total Quality Initiatives as ineffective. Flow charts of the existing process become an important tool in aiding group members in visualizing the simplification which is possible by eliminating and paralleling steps in the process.

Scatter diagrams are very useful in providing a clear, simple picture of relationships between data—particularly cause-and-effect correlations.

All of these metrics allow a group to demonstrate progress toward its next destination. High Performance teamwork hastens the dispersal of information throughout all levels of the organization. The fact is *when a group fails to mature to High Performance Work, the cause is often a lack of progress metrics, or poorly defined goals* that don't readily lend themselves to measurement.

Figure 10-3A

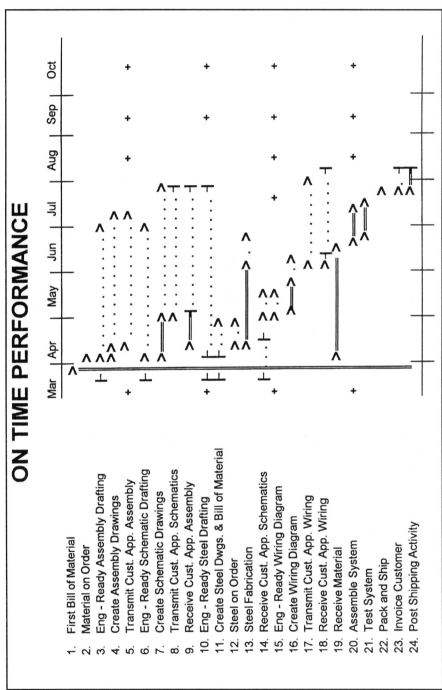

Figure 10-3B

ANALYZING DATA: Force-Field Analysis

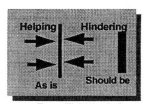

Force-Field Analysis

What Force-Field Analysis Is

Developed by the organizational researcher Kurt Lewin, force-field analysis identifies those forces that both help and hinder you from closing the gap between where you are now and where you want to be.

What Force-Field Analysis Looks Like

Figure 10-4 is a force-field analysis completed by a group working on the problem "Morale in this department is low. "

How to Use Force-Field Analysis

- Draw a line down the center of a flip chart page. This represents the "as-is" situation—what currently exists. (This should be very similar to your statement of the problem.)

- At the right edge of the sheet, draw a second vertical line parallel to the first. This represents the situation as it should be (the desired state).

- Using one or more of the tools for collecting and generating information, identify and list the helping forces to the left of the center line, the hindering forces to the right of the center line.

These "forces" are often shown as arrows: The helping forces are pushing toward the "should-be" state and the hindering forces are pushing away from it.

It's often helpful to assess the relative strengths of both helping and hindering forces. Some groups use a scale (e.g., 5 = very strong, 4 = strong, 3 = medium, 2 = low, 1 = weak) to evaluate the relative impact of the forces. For graphic representation, proportionately sized arrows show relative strengths.

Once the analysis is complete, your group can use this information to generate potential solutions. Some ideas that the group can explore:

- How to increase the number or strength of the helping forces.
- How to decrease the number or strength of the hindering forces.

Reprinted from **Quality Tools and Techniques**, ABB Institute

FORCE-FIELD ANALYSIS

STATEMENT OF THE PROBLEM
Morale in this department is low.

GOAL
Department members rate morale as 4 or higher.

AS IS	SHOULD BE
Helping	**Hindering**
Cooperation within the department	Inconsistent recognition
———>	<———
Communications meetings	No second-level performance reviews
———>	<——
Quarterly recognition program	No pre-management development
———>	<——
Problem solving teams established	No sourcing procedures
——————>	<———————
	Managers not involved in problem solving
	<———

Figure 10-4

ANALYZING AND DISPLAYING DATA: PARETO ANALYSIS

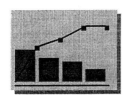

What Pareto Analysis Is

Pareto analysis is a technique that separates the "vital few" from the "trivial many." Named for Vilfredo Pareto, a 19th-century Italian economist who did work with income and other unequal distributions, a Pareto analysis is designed to point out inequalities.

The familiar 80-20 rule ("Eighty percent of our business comes from twenty percent of our customers") is an example of Pareto analysis.

The basic concept behind a Pareto analysis involves the ranking of data, and the analysis is usually presented in a Pareto diagram. Like a histogram (or bar graph), a Pareto analysis shows a distribution. The bars, however, are arranged in descending order of frequency or magnitude from left to right.

A Pareto analysis (or diagram) is used to draw attention to problems (or causes) in a systematic way. It shows which are the greatest problems, thereby enabling a group to set priorities.

Pareto diagrams may be used with or without a cumulative line. When cumulative lines are used, they represent the percentage sum of the vertical bars, as if they were stacked on each other going from left to right.

What a Pareto Diagram Looks Like

The next two pages describe a Pareto analysis prepared by a HPWS group. Group members fabricate integrated circuit (IC) boards.

How to Make a Pareto Diagram

- Use a check sheet to collect the required data.
- Arrange the data in order from largest category to smallest.

- Calculate the total.
- Compute the percent of the total that each category represents.
- Compute the cumulative percent. (See example below.)
- Draw horizontal and vertical axes on graph paper.
- Scale the vertical axis for frequency (0 to total calculated above).
- Working from left to right, construct a bar for each category, with height indicating the frequency. Start with the largest category and add them in descending order.
- Draw a vertical scale on the right of the graph and add percent scale (0% to 100%).
- Plot the cumulative percent lines as shown below.

Pareto diagrams have become a valuable tool in industry because they identify the main sources of variation. Consider the analysis the HPWS group put together. After the IC boards are fabricated, certain tests are made to determine if the boards meet the shipping specifications. Of all the IC boards determined not to meet the quality specifications, it was found that the following defect types contributed to rejecting the final product: soldering, etching, molding, cracking, and a last category that is labeled "other." A Pareto diagram for this defect data is shown in Figure 10-5.

While the left vertical axis of Figure 10-5 shows the actual number of defects, the right vertical axis represents the cumulative percent frequency of defects and is a convenient scale from which to read the line graph. The line graph connects the points which represent the cumulative (from left to right) heights of the bars. The use of both a frequency axis and a percent axis conveys more information to the decision maker than the use of just a frequency axis or percent axis alone.

Figure 10-5 clearly indicates that about 65% of the defects arise from faulty soldering or etching and that perhaps management may want to concentrate its defect removal efforts in these areas. However, a few words of caution are in order. While faulty soldering is the leading culprit as far as number of defects is concerned, it may not be the leading source for loss of revenue. In fact, etching defects require a greater amount of rework than do soldering defects and, as such, represent a greater amount of monetary loss. Hence, a Pareto diagram showing the amount of lost revenue may appear as in Figure 10-6 and might be more applicable than Figure 10-5.

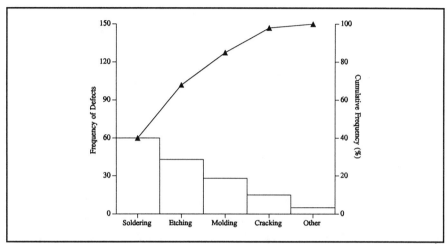

Figure 10-5 Pareto Diagram of IC Board Defects

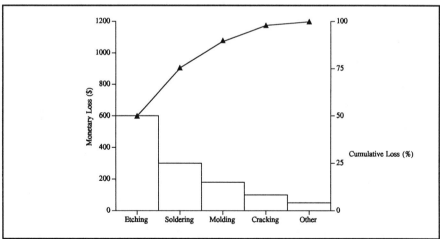

Figure 10-6 Pareto Diagram of Defects vs Monetary Loss

A Pareto diagram such as that in Figure 10-6, which shows that two kinds of defects account for 75 percent of the losses, is clearly a useful tool.

Taken from the book Basic Statistics: Tools for Continuous Improvement
By Mark J. Kiemele & Stephen R. Schmidt
Air Academy Press & Associates, CO

ANALYZING DATA: Cause-and-Effect Diagram
(Also referred to as an Ishikawa Diagram or Fishbone)

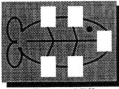

Cause-and-Effect

What Cause-and-Effect Diagrams Are
Like Pareto analysis, this analysis is usually shown diagrammatically. Cause-and-effect diagrams are also known as fishbones (because of their shape) or Ishikawa diagrams, after their inventor, Dr. Kaoru Ishikawa, a Japanese quality control statistician.

Cause-and-effect analysis is a systematic way of identifying, displaying and examining effects and the causes that create or contribute to those effects. The effects can be either problems (the "as is" statement of the situation you want to correct) or desired states (what you want to exist when problems have been solved).

What Cause-and-Effect Diagrams Look Like

The cause-and-effect diagram in Figure 10-7 is based on an example developed by a subgroup in training to demonstrate the use of a specific tool. The "as-is" problem statement, "LOW GAS MILEAGE," appears at the head. The bones represent the major causes that could explain why the gas mileage is lower than desired.

How to Use Cause-and-Effect Diagrams

- Decide on the effect to be analyzed and write it on the right end of a board or large sheet of paper—the fish's head.
- Draw a horizontal line from the head across the paper, with several "major bones" drawn on a slant.
  - Write the main factors which contribute to the effect at the ends of the major bones.
  - For the technical problems, the factors Man, Machine, Materials, Method, and Environment are frequently used.
  - For sales problems, the factors People, Product, Price, and Promotion may be useful.

- On each of the major bones, write the specific factors that the group considers to be causes. The group may use brainstorming or other data collection methods to identify these.
- Identify the most significant factor (or combination of factors); collect additional data to verify causal relationship to effect.

CAUSE-AND-EFFECT DIAGRAM

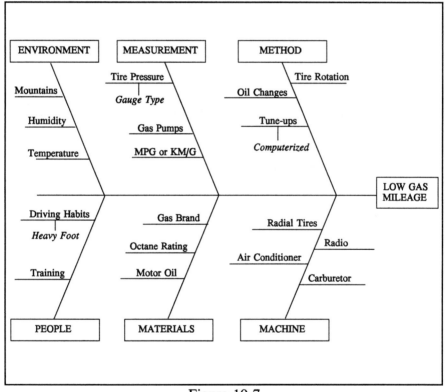

Figure 10-7

Taken from the book Basic Statistics: Tools for Continuous Improvement
By Mark J. Kiemele & Stephen R. Schmidt
Air Academy Press & Associates, CO

TOOLS FOR PLANNING ACTIONS: GANTT CHARTS

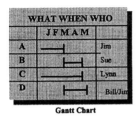

Gantt Chart

What a Gantt Chart is

A Gantt chart is a diagram that documents schedule, events, activities, and responsibilities necessary to complete a project or to implement a group's proposed solution.

What a Gantt Chart Looks Like

The form on the next page (Figure 10-8) is an example. (Although there are many variations, all Gantt charts document what is to be accomplished, by whom, and when.) This chart also allows a group to document the assumptions underlying their implementation plan. For example, if the plan is based on installation of equipment by May 15, that assumption can be noted. The group can then develop contingency plans in case that deadline slips past.

How to Use a Gantt Chart

• Break the implementation plan into achievable steps.

• Assign responsibility for each step to a group member.

• Decide how long each task will take and set a realistic completion date.

• Document the assumptions on which the plan is based and the contingency plans to implement if those assumptions are not valid.

SAMPLE GANTT CHART

Assumptions	Week Ending							

SCHEDULE								
Task	Assigned To	Week Ending						

Reprinted from Quality Tools and Techniques, ABB Institute

Figure 10-8

Tools for Planning Actions: Process Maps

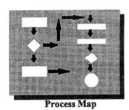

Process Map

What Process Maps Are

A process map shows the inputs, activities, decision points, and outputs for a given process. Its purpose is to pictorially display the process as it actually exists. Programmers and analysts make extensive use of this tool to document the logic of computer programs.

What a Process Map Looks Like

The construction of a process map should use a minimum number of easily interpreted symbols. Three different shaped objects, together with arrows connecting the objects to denote direction of flow, are usually sufficient to construct a good process map.

How to Construct a Process Map

Process maps use standard symbols connected by arrows to show how the system or work process operates. To construct a process map, identify the major activities to be completed and decisions to be made as the recommended solution is implemented. Then check the logic of the plan by following all possible routes through the chart to ensure that you have planned for contingencies. Figure 10-9 depicts three shapes that are commonly used, as well as their implied meanings.

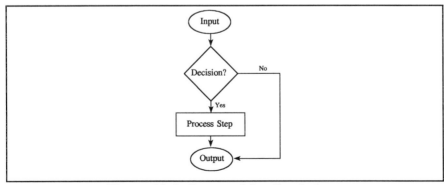

Figure 10-9 Process Map Symbology

When to Use Process Maps

Process maps are particularly useful for documenting the contingencies —and contingency plans—that may arise during the course of implementing the recommended solution.

Almost every process or system that needs to be studied can be represented by a process map (or a flow chart). Further, the level of detail that is needed can be easily adjusted by replacing a process step at one level of detail, for example, with a more detailed chart that is representative of a lower level of abstraction. Hence, the flow chart is a graphical tool that allows the practitioner the ability to describe the steps in a process in as much detail as necessary. Obviously, the box labeled "Consult Manual" in Figure 10-10 could have its own flow chart which conceivably could be many times as large as Figure 10-10 itself. Flow charts should be carefully evaluated to identify non-value added steps to be removed from a process and to identify areas that could be addressed to improve quality. An example of a non-value added step in Figure 10-10 is the box labeled "Plug Power Cord In." In a "quality" process, this is a step that should not have to be accomplished over and over again.

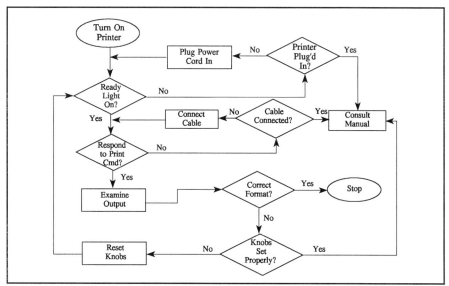

Figure 10-10 Process Map: Operation of a Computer Printer

Taken from Basic Statistics: Tools for Continuous Improvement. Air Academy Press.

ANALYZING DATA: SCATTER DIAGRAMS

What a Scatter Diagram Is

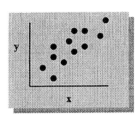

The relationship between two kinds of paired data, i.e., the cause and the effect, can be plotted on a chart known as a scatter diagram. The purpose of constructing a scatter diagram is to study and visually depict and quantify the relationship between two variables. The diagram does not prove that one variable causes the other but it does make it clear whether a relationship exists and the strength of that relationship.

What a Scatter Diagram Looks Like

A scatter diagram includes a horizontal axis (x-axis), representing the measurement values of one variable, and the vertical axis (y-axis), representing the measurements of the second variable. The plotted points generally form a clustered pattern. The direction and tightness of the cluster gives you a clue as to the strength of the relationship between variable 1 and variable 2. The more the cluster resembles a straight line, the stronger the relationship between the two variables.

The correct reading of a scatter diagram is necessary for proper action. To help you correctly read a scatter diagram, the following samples of the most common scatter diagrams are shown below.

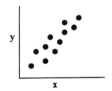

Positive correlation
An increase in y depends on increases in x. If x is controlled, y naturally will be controlled.

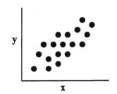

Positive correlation may be present

If x increases, y will increase somewhat, but y seems to have causes other than x.

How to Read a Scatter Diagram

No correlation

There is no correlation.

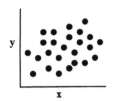

Negative correlation may be present

An increase in x will cause a tendency for a decrease in y.

Negative correlation

An increase in x will cause a decrease in y. Therefore, as with positive correlation, x may be controlled instead of y.

When correlation does exist, it is often helpful to know its extent. With the help of a statistician, the coefficient of correlation can be calculated using the binomial probability paper or the median method of analyzing correlations. (See also *Guide to Quality Control* by Kaoru Ishikawa.)

Reprinted from Quality Tools and Techniques. ABB Institute

Epilogue

You have reached the end of the book, but *now is when your journey truly begins*. I have tried to capture in each of the chapters of *Beyond Survival* the essence of the steps required to achieve High Performance in your organization. The book is not a complete guide to this process; a book many times thicker could not contain all of the information available on developing High Performance Work! But I hope I have stimulated your interest, captured your imagination, and convinced you that **High Performance is necessary, worthwhile,** and **achievable** in your work environment.

Now you must take the next step. Perhaps you'll begin on a small scale to implement the concepts covered in this book. When you're ready to take a more all-encompassing approach to High Performance in your organization there are many excellent texts, process tools, and dynamic and talented individuals in the Human Resource and Quality Management fields to be tapped as resources for that challenge.

Human Capital Associates provides consulting services in the building of High Performance Groups. My publisher, Air Academy Press & Associates, in addition to providing many texts which address the tools required to achieve quality processes, also provides consulting and training services.

Today, there is no organization which cannot benefit from the implementation of High Performance Work Systems. Join me in this challenging, ever-changing growth process and reap the benefits of reaching *Beyond Survival* and *Creating Prosperity Through People*.

The author

Seven Arrows Ranch
Colorado

May, 1995

Glossary

Action Steps:

Detailed plans for achieving goals and objectives, divided into events and actions necessary to make the goal or objective achievable. They must be measurable and measured.

Agenda:

A list of the issues and items to be discussed in a meeting. They will have specific assigned times and accountabilities.

Autonomy:

An individual's or group's authority to make decisions and to control what and how things are done. Autonomy is never absolute; it exists within the limits of expressed "boundaries."

Brainstorming:

A free-form approach to generating ideas and options that can be useful in developing an action plan. Participants are encouraged to express any and all ideas freely without censoring or judging themselves or each other.

Organization Culture:

The conscious and unconscious mission, goals, principles and rules which dictate organizational behavior and attitudes. "What it feels like" to live in a specific organization.

Consensus:

General agreement by a group on how an issue is to be resolved. Consensus does not imply unanimity. It is achieved when most members are in agreement and those who differ, having expressed their choices, commit themselves to supporting the decision.

Continuous Improvement: The idea that improvement is a never-ending process is central to High Performance thinking. The attainment of goals does not mean that the effort to improve ceases.

Critique: A review of actions and behaviors for the purpose of helping or improving.

Decision Matrix: A graphic method for displaying organization decision making guidelines for various categories or types of decisions. The decision levels are displayed on a grid with each vertical column representing an increasing or decreasing level of decision-making. The horizontal columns represent types of categories or decisions.

Employee Involvement: A philosophy of management where employees are encouraged and allowed to make decisions about work and organization.

Facilitation: Assistance of others to accomplish objectives.

Facilitator: An individual who assumes a behavioral leadership role for assisting a group of people working on a common objective.

Gap Analysis: A formal comparison of a group's current status and where it wants to be.

Goals: The end results toward which an organization strives. Goals provide structured guidance toward accomplishing the mission; they are generally strategic in nature and have a 1-3-year time frame.

Greenfield Site: A new opportunity or "start up," presenting great latitude in implementing structural or design concepts.

Ground Rules: Rules defining acceptable and unacceptable actions and behavior for team members. Ground rule violations should be addressed immediately.

Group Centered Meeting: A meeting in which each member of the group has responsibility for achieving a successful outcome. Member interaction and needs have a profound effect on task solution and, therefore, need to be understood and addressed.

High Performance: A sustained level of outcomes far above industry standards, providing the organization with a competitive advantage.

Leader-Centered Meeting: A meeting in which the leader is responsible for directing, driving, instructing, and controlling the group. The leader's task is to get the job done quickly and efficiently.

Linkages: The connections (person to person) to the service or management support required to regulate boundaries; such as Purchasing, Maintenance, etc.

Metrics: A formal system of performance measures which are closely followed and usually tied to goals.

Mission: A statement defining the organization's unique purpose. It should answer the questions: Who are we? What do we do? For whom do we do it? and Why do we do it?

Natural Work Team: A work group with interdependent activities that are focused on a specific project or process with a definable beginning and end.

Norms: The "normal" expectations a group places on its members regarding behavior and responses. A single violation of a norm usually doesn't warrant immediate action. Repeated violations can be disruptive and counterproductive, and should be addressed.

Objectives: What must be achieved in support of strategies to accomplish goals. Objectives are measurable and generally have a 12-18-month time frame.

Paradigms: A set of rules and regulations (conscious and unconscious) that define boundaries for behavior, opinions, and decision-making. (Strongly held paradigms/rules act as filters to screen information coming in.) People tend to select the information that best suits their "paradigms" and ignore the rest.

Participative Management: A new approach to organizational management, wherein power, knowledge, information, and rewards are moved to lower levels of the organization, giving people power to influence matters that affect them.

Performance Measures: The tracking and quantification of results over time that are indicators of individual or group performance. They are usually tracked against a goal or target.

Problem Solving:

A formal group process for identifying solutions and creating desired changes.

Problem-Solving Group:

An ad-hoc group of employees, trained in problem-solving techniques and group processes. These groups study and analyze issues and make recommendations for improvement.

Process:

Any series of related tasks, actions, or steps designed to achieve a desired product or outcome.

Quorum:

The minimum number of members that must be present before the group can transact business and make decisions. A majority.

Redesign:

Changes and improvements in the organization or work system design.

Resource:

A supply of anything a team can draw upon to enhance its capabilities and perform better. Resources include cash, talent, raw materials, etc.

Role:

A function or office assumed by someone in order to play a necessary part in a group activity.

Self-Regulated:

Describing a group of individuals working together to mutually resolve and coordinate activities and requirements to fully satisfy their mission.

Self-Regulated Work:

A group of employees within an organization who have decision-making authority over various issues and actions, within agreed-upon "boundaries."

Socio-Technical Redesign: Changing or redesigning a work system by analyzing and determining the needs of the people who do the work, as well as the technical aspects of the work process.

System: A group of related processes that work together to create a product or achieve some other desired result.

Team Boundaries: The limits of decision-making within understood areas of responsibility (i.e. assigned space or facilities to operate within, people to contact for decisions, actions that require involvement outside of department, etc.).

Team Structure: An organizational framework of behavioral guidelines and expectations.

Trust: An indispensable ingredient in any High Performance undertaking. Trust is based on perceived commitments and individuals' codes of honor. It is hard to obtain, easy to lose, and priceless in any organization.

Vision: Ideals, hopes, and dreams that are held in hearts and minds. It is these larger dreams that bring meaning to what we do. For the organization it provides a backdrop for its reason for being.

Addendum

SKILL DIMENSIONS IN THE HIGH PERFORMANCE WORK SYSTEM

Required Skill Dimensions Associated with High Performance Work Systems: The process of identifying competence and potential should focus on the assessment of individual competence utilizing these *Skill Dimensions*:

1) **Leadership**
   Influences the actions and opinions of others in a desired direction; exhibits judgment in leading others to worthwhile objectives.

2) **Followship**
   Readily assumes a "team member" role and contributes to the team's success without over-concern for "self."

3) **Decisiveness**
   Makes decisions based on available information and takes action; makes commitments and does not change decisions when challenged (unless presented with new, compelling information). Makes tough decisions in terms of both work and people.

4) **Coping**
   Maintains a mature problem solving attitude while dealing with interpersonal conflict, hazardous conditions, personal rejection, hostility, or time demands; able to balance personal and professional commitments.

5) **Creativity**
   Develops unique and novel solutions to problems; presents information in an attention-gaining and interesting manner.

6) **Versatility**
   Modifies behavioral style to respond to the needs of others while maintaining focus on business objectives.

7) **Decision Making/Judgment**
Identifies the important dimensions of a problem, determines potential causes, obtains relevant information, and specifies alternatives.

8) **Persuasiveness**
Uses appropriate interpersonal style and methods of communication to obtain agreement or acceptance of an idea, plan, activity, or product.

9) **Commitment**
Exhibits dedication to the company and career; willing to occasionally work long hours when necessary and make personal sacrifices to advance the business and accomplish objectives.

BIBLIOGRAPHY/REFERENCE

1. *The Journal of Business Strategy,* Spring 1983

2. *Sloan Management Review,* Fall 1984

3. "Coming to a New Awareness of Organizational Culture," *Sloan Reprint Series,* Winter 1984

4. "Organizational Dynamics," *AMA,* Winter 1979

5. "Team Development Growth Process," Saturn Corporation

6. "Managing in a Team Environment," Xerox Corporation

7. Katzenbach, Smith, "The Wisdom of Teams," *Harvard Business School Press,* 1993

8. "Partnership at Saturn Corporation," *MIT Management,* Spring 1992

9. General Electric Annual Report, February 14, 1992

10. Miller Brewing Company Whitepaper, June 4, 1992

11. Bruce Rayner, "Trial-by-Fire Transformation: An Interview with Globe Metallurgical's Arden C. Sims," *Harvard Business Review,* May-June 1992

12. Steve Rayner & Kim Fisher, "Creating a High Performance Team," Eastman Kodak

13. "New Rules For Managers Parts I through II," *Work in America Institute National Policy Study*

14. David A. Garvin, "How the Baldrige Award Really Works," *Harvard Business Review,* November-December 1991

15. James L. Broadhead, "The Post-Deming Diet," *Training,* February 1991

16. "Self Directed Work Teams," <u>Business One Irwin 1990</u>. Orsburn, Moral, Musserwhite and Fonger

17. *Corporate Cultures,* Deal & Kennedy, Addison Wesley, October 1990

18. *Organizational Transitions,* Beckhard & Harris, Addison Wesley O.D. Series, 1987

19. "Concepts of the Saturn Organization, Phase II," Saturn Corporation

20. "The Search for the Organization of Tomorrow," *Fortune,* May 18, 1992

21. "A Design & Philosophy for Empowerment," *Miller Brewing Company,* June 1992

22. General Mills Review, Second Quarter 1992

23. "New Work Systems," *New Choices Labor Relations Today,* March/April 1991

24. "A High Involvement Redesign," *Sociotechnical Systems,* 1990

25. "Views on Self-Directed Workteams from the Line to the Front Office," *Journal for Quality and Participation,* December 1990

26. "From the Plant Up," *Enterprise,* Summer 1990

27. "Who Needs a Boss?," *Fortune,* May 7, 1990

28. "Topeka Revisited," *Human Resource Executive,* May 1990

29. "Self-Managed Work Teams Score for Insurance Company," *National Productivity Report,* January 31, 1990

30. "Creating a High-Performance Team: Eastman Kodak's 13 Room Belgard," Fisher, Rayner, Inc. 1990

31. "The Team Book," *Sherwin Williams Automotive Plan*

32. *Empowered Teams - Creating Self-Directed Work Groups That Improve Quality, Productivity, and Participation,* Richard S. Wellins, William C. Byham, and Jeanne M. Wilson, Jossey-Bass Inc., 1991

33. *Work Redesign,* by J. Richard Hackman, Yale University and Greg R. Oldham, University of Illinois, Addison-Wesley Publishing Co., 1980

34. *Corporate Transformation - Revitalizing Organizations for a Competitive World,* Ralph H. Kilmann, Teresa Joyce Covin, and Associates, Jossey-Bass Inc., Publishers

35. *Large-Scale Organizational Change,* Allan M. Mohrman, Jr., Susan Albers Mohrman, Gerald E. Ledford,Jr., Thomas G. Cummings, Edward E. Lawler III, and Associates, Jossey-Bass Inc., Publishers, 1989

36. *Productive Workplaces - Organizing and Managing for Dignity, Meaning, and Community,* Marvin R. Weisbord, Jossey-Bass Inc., Publishers, 1987

37. *High-Involvement Management - Participative Strategies for Improving Organizational Performance,* Edward E. Lawler III, Jossey-Bass Inc., Publishers, 1986

38. *Groups That Work (and Those That Don't) - Creating Conditions for Effective Teamwork.* J. Richard Hackman, Jossey-Bass Inc., Publishers, 1990

39. *Managerial Psychology,* Harold J. Leavitt, Fourth Edition, University of Chicago Press, 1979

40. *The Human Side of Just-In-Time,* Charlene Adair-Heeley, AMACON, 1991

41.   *World Class Manufacturing,* Richard J. Schonberger, The Free Press, 1986

42.   *Japanese Manufacturing Techniques*, Richard J. Schonberger, The Free Press

43.   *Structured Teamwork, A Market Driven Process,* Performance Resources. Inc.,

44.   *TeamBuilt,* Dave Sanborn

45.   *Creating The High Performance Team,* Steve Buchholz and Thomas Roth

46.   *The Adventures of a Self-Managing Team,* Mark Kelly

47.   Jerome Rosow & Robert Zager, "New Roles for Managers," *Work in America*

48.   "New Work Systems, New Choices in Labor Relations," U.S. Dept. of Labor, Lynn Marlin, Secretary

49.   Amy J. Katz, Patricia Laughlin, Jeanne Wilson, "Views on Self-Directed Work Teams from the Line to the Front Office," *Journal for Quality and Participation,* December 1990

50.   Richard J. Magjuka, "Survey: Self Managed Teams Achieve Continuous Improvement Best," *National Productivity Review,* Winter 1991/92

51.   *High Involvement Management,* Edward Lawler III

52.   *Designing Organizations for High Performance,* David P. Hanna, Addison - Wesley

53.   *Essentials of Major Change,* Steven Rayner, BFR

54.   "Vision, Opportunity and Tenacity: Three Informal Processes that Influence Formal Transformation," William P. Belgard, K. Kim Fisher, Steven Rayner; Extract from Corporate Transformation Ed. by Kilman, R.H., and Covin, T.J., Jossey-Bass, 1988

55.   *Pathways to High Involvement,* Steven Rayner, BFR

56.   Peter Senge, "The Leader's New World: Building Learning Organizations," *Sloan Management Review,* Fall 1990

57.   Jana Schilder, "Work Teams Boost Productivity," *Personnel Journal,* February 1992

58.   "STS Design," Beth Waller, Jim Taylor, Tom Christensen; Proceedings of the Quality of Life/Marketing Conference, Virginia Polytechnic Institute, November 10, 1989

59.   *Championship Management*, James A. Belohlav

60.   Brian Dumaine, "Who needs a Boss?," *Fortune,* May 7, 1990

61.   Chris Lee, "Beyond Teamwork," *Training,* June 1990

62.   "Organization Change and Work Innovation: A Meta - Analysis of 131 North American Field Experiments, 1961-1990," Barry Macy, Paul D. Bliese, Joseph J. Norton; 1991 National Academy of Management Meeting, Miami Florida, August 11 - 14, 1991

63.   General Mills Annual Report 1991

64.   General Electric Annual Report 1991

65.   *The Quiet Revolution,* A. Micossi, Digital Equipment Corporation

66.   K. Kim Fisher, "Management Roles in the Implementation of Participative Management Systems," *Human Resource Management,* Fall 1986 Vol. 25 No. 3

67.   *The STS Design Handbook,* Erickson, Walton Trist, Naisbitt & Others, STS Publishing

68.   Robert Janson and Jerry Laubenstein, "Self Managed Teams Score for Insurance Company," *National Productivity Report,* January 31, 1990, Volume 19 No.2

69.   Michael Donovan, "Redesigning the Workplace," *Journal for Quality and Participation,* December 1989

70.   K. Kim Fisher, "Managing in the High Commitment Workplace," *Organizational Dynamics,* Winter 1989

71.   Ikujiro Nonaka, "The Knowledge Creating Company," *Harvard Business Review,* November- December 1991

72.   Beverly Geber, "Saturn's Grand Experiment," *Training,* June 1992

73.   Robert M. Schaffer and Harvey A. Thomson, "Successful Change Programs Begin with Results," *Harvard Business Review,* January-February 1992

74.   Richard L. Bunning, "Skill Based Pay," *Personnel Administrator,* June 1989

75.   "New Ways to Pay," *The Economist,* July 13, 1991

76.   B. McWilliams, "New Rewards for New York," *Enterprize,* Winter 1991/92

77.   K. Dave Scott and Timothy Colter, "Teams That Work Together Earn Together," *Personnel Journal,* March 1984

78.   "Pay for Knowledge Pays Off, *Labor Relations Today,* July-August 1991

79. Kenneth Labich, "The New Pay Game and How You Measure Up," *Fortune,* October 19, 1992

80. Charles Handy, "The Age of Unreason," *Harvard Business School Press*

81. *Even Eagles Need a Push,* David McNally, Delacorte Press

82. *Managing Transitions,* William Bridges, Addison Wesley

83. *Surviving Corporate Transitions,* William Bridges, William Bridges and Assoc.

84. *Teaching the Elephant to Dance,* James A. Belaco, Penguin Books

85. "Designing the Learning Organization," Peter Senge, 1992 Conference of Organizational System Designers

86. "Accelerating Change through Open Book Management," Jack Stack, 1992 Conference of Organizational System Designers

87. "Teamwork at the Top: The Senior Management Team at Weyerhaeuser," Charles Bingham and Steve Hill, New Roles in the Workplace Work in America Roundtable, October 20-23, 1992, Scottsdale, AZ

88. "GE Capital Corporation: The Changing Role of the Managers/Team Developer," Mary Allen, Adi Westenhofer, et al; New Roles in the Workplace Work in America Roundtable, October 20-23, 1992, Scottsdale, AZ

89. "Creating a New Culture for Union Management Relations at Magma Copper," Marsh Campbell, Don Shelton, et al; New Roles in the Workplace Work in America Roundtable, October 20-23, 1992, Scottsdale, AZ

90. *The Great Game of Business,* Jack Stack, Doubleday

91. *Basic Statistics: Tools for Continuous Improvement,* 3rd edition, Mark J. Kiemele and Stephen R. Schmidt, Air Academy Press, Colorado Springs, CO, 1993.

NOTES

NOTES

For more information on
HUMAN CAPITAL ASSOCIATES
or the author
write to:

HUMAN CAPITAL ASSOCIATES
c/o ROBERT BLAHA
14335 ROLLER COASTER RD.
COLORADO SPRINGS, CO 80921